THE
MOMENTUM
of HOPE

THE MOMENTUM
of HOPE
PERSONAL STORIES OF MORAL INJURY

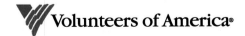

Volunteers of America®

CONTENTS

FOREWORD

IF THERE HAD BEEN ANY UNDERSTANDING about moral injury when I was in my twenties, my life would have been much easier, my father's life would have been easier. If I could have read the stories shared in "A Momentum of Hope," I would have had the knowledge and insight to better understand and empathize with my Army Colonel father, the youngest of 18 children from rural Louisiana, who fought in World War II, Korea, and Vietnam. I would have known that, as he heroically waded through the sludge of unspeakable racism, atrocities, the death of my mother at 37 and memories of killing, he left some of himself behind with each invisible injury. All the symptoms were there but I didn't know . . . he didn't know.

My father and my family suffered the consequences of his moral injuries.

While most of the stories in this book depict the emptiness and vagueness that come from feeling inadequate, unlovable or unworthy, the writers ultimately find ways to cope, recover, or heal. So much of their healing involves friends, families, and communities of faith who listened, believed, and didn't judge. In order to tell a story, someone must listen.

Being able to share a profoundly personal story of moral injury is essential to the recovery process. We are grateful to the people who contributed their stories to this book and hope that their candor and generosity helps readers better understand moral injury and its impact.

Moral injury is the consequence of violations to our core moral convictions. Whatever is done is of such harm that it negates our moral expectations of ourselves and others. The shared moral covenant that sustains meaningful relationships between individuals and their world is lost.

It can also be a self-inflicted wound. When we violate our own moral code, witness such transgressions, or fail to stop harm, we judge ourselves negatively and suffer.

The suffering of moral injury is characterized by guilt or shame, emotional isolation, and a loss of trust. Violations can come from being betrayed by those in power who fail to do the right thing, especially in high-stakes situations.

At the time of our founding in 1896, Volunteers of America first encountered the emotional aftermath of war on veterans who served in the Civil War. We have been committed to the well-being of those who served our country and their families ever since. In recent years, the spike in veteran suicide led us to embrace the concept of moral injury and launch a new initiative to help provide relief and a means to recovery for those suffering from moral injury. Our search for a path to healing started with veterans, and also includes long-term caregivers and victims of sexual assault, discrimination, and other experiences that may cause trauma.

Thank you to HSBC for their generous support of Volunteers of America's work in the area of moral injury, and their commitment to the veterans and others who have experienced the devastating effects of moral injury. We hope these stories will open your eyes, and your hearts, to the people in your family, faith communities, and circles of friends who are suffering and working to recover from the anguish of moral injury.

JATRICE MARTEL GAITER
Co-editor

PUTTING THIS BOOK TOGETHER was an eye-opening (and mind-opening) experience. Gathering these vivid and deeply personal stories made me marvel at the strength and resilience of the human spirit. The individuals who shared their tales of trauma, tragedy, and violence lived through some incredibly difficult and trying times and emerged able to move on with their lives. Perhaps even more extraordinary is the fact that so many of them then made it their life's work to help others in need.

We gathered these stories from a wide variety of sources. The individuals who contributed essays to *The Momentum of Hope* are caregivers, civil rights activists, first responders, veterans, scholars, academics, members of the faith community, and more. They're a very diverse group hailing from big cities and small towns across the United States. As you read these stories, you'll see that moral injury can afflict anyone, regardless of education, economic status, or professional success.

It is our hope that you will be as moved as we were by these personal accounts and that you will gain a deeper understanding of moral injury. Our work in this field is just beginning, and we look forward to continuing to raise awareness and to address the challenges of moral injury.

DOUGLAS McALLISTER
Co-editor

CONTINUING THE GOOD FIGHT

MIKE KING

Volunteers of America represents the caregivers and the healers. We are an organization that serves veterans, those coming out of incarceration, and those being healed from addiction—all who have experienced moral injury in their own ways.

But there is another group of folks who suffer in similar ways yet tend to live in the shadows: the caregivers. The caregivers of those we serve. The caregivers who see failure more than they see success and who experience that failure on a deep level. The caregivers who tend to others who are not going to get well, such as those drifting into the abyss of Alzheimer's and other dementia-related disorders. The caregivers who struggle to provide care, knowing they won't win.

 I came to know moral injury on a personal level during my experience as the caregiver for my mom in the last several years of her life. My mother was little, hardheaded and tough—they make them that way in Texas, especially when they're hairdressers! She ran her own beauty parlor business in an era when few women worked outside of the home. I grew up thinking Aqua Net was air freshener. My mother was the toughest person I ever knew. You have to be tough if you're going to get through three stillborn babies to get to me. And yet, as I cared for her toward the end of her life, I realized we couldn't win this battle.

I visited my mother two days a week and provided housekeeping services for her three days a week. I made sure she would never have to live at a nursing facility so she could live independently, the way she wanted to. But, as I cared for her, I began doubting my own strength. "Why can't I sacrifice more?" I wondered. "Why don't I put my job on the backburner? Why don't I do what I know she would have done for me at a critical time?" Even now, more than a decade later, I never wake up in the morning feeling as if I did everything I could for my mother. Not ever. I never wake up thinking I was a good son.

It wasn't until I heard other caregivers tell their stories that I realized we all suffer from the same moral injury—the feeling that we didn't follow our own moral values when it counted most. How could we not have done more for our loved one? I also realized we are all seeking validation in what we had done to try to repair our wounded soul that we will carry with us the rest of our lives. Everyone who provides care for someone who passes experiences this. Every surviving spouse experiences this. So, yes, moral injury exists. I can tell you firsthand, moral injury is real. The need for soul care is present.

I'm proud to lead an organization like Volunteers of America, which has been at the forefront of serving people with moral injury from its inception and at a time when people didn't even know what to call moral injury. When Volunteers of America was founded in 1896—30 years after the end of the Civil War—the United States faced an epidemic of moral injury that rarely gets discussed in history lessons. Most veterans who fought in the Civil War were in their 40s and 50s by the end of the 19th Century and many remained overwhelmed by the devastation of the war, where 625,000 Americans lost their lives on their home soil.

So imagine, if you will, a country divided in 1896—divided politically, and divided racially. It had only been about 30 years since the end of slavery and, in many ways, we were still fighting those battles. While the smoke from the worst conflict in our history was still clearing, the founders of Volunteers of America were still serving Civil War veterans daily through prison ministry, substance abuse work, spiritual guidance, and in shelters and soup lines.

> "My mother was little, hardheaded and tough—they make them that way in Texas, especially when they're hairdressers!"

The term "post-traumatic stress disorder" had not yet been coined, but no war was as personal or intimate in battle as the Civil War. Soldiers weren't fighting in a foreign land, and they weren't fighting people they didn't know. Battles were sometimes fought by hand and often between people who knew one another. It was trauma on steroids. And that's the root of post-traumatic stress disorder (PTSD)— exposure to trauma and the effect it has on the brain. The term moral injury directly relates to this type of hurt; it's what happens to the soul after a person participates in an act they were raised to believe is wrong.

This is how Volunteers of America defines moral injury:

"Moral injury results when someone violates their core moral beliefs, and in evaluating their behavior negatively they believe they no longer live in a reliable, meaningful world, and they can no longer be regarded as decent human beings. They may even feel this after what they did was warranted and unavoidable. Killing, torturing, abusing, and failing to prevent such acts can illicit moral injury. Veterans' affairs clinicians have started to see moral injury as separate from PTSD and as a hidden wound of war. The consequences of violating one's conscience, even if the act was unavoidable or perceived right at the time, can be devastating. Responses include overwhelming depression, guilt, and self-medication through alcohol or drugs. Moral injury can lead veterans to feelings of worthlessness, remorse, and despair. They may feel as if they lost their souls in combat

"Even now, more than a decade later, I never wake up in the morning feeling as if I did every-thing I could for my mother."

and are no longer who they were. Connecting to others becomes impossible for those trapped inside those feelings. When these consequences become overwhelming, the only relief may seem to be to leave this life behind."

Think about the conditions of the Civil War, then consider what happened in the decades that followed. Most of the people Volunteers of America was serving at the time were suffering from some form of moral injury. I wonder how many service people today—veterans or otherwise—are also suffering from moral injury? People who feel they have lost their soul due to a regrettable act and who wish they could wipe the act away but their minds won't let them.

I think we have the opportunity today to examine what our Volunteers of America forebears started and the challenges they faced. We also have more research and resources at our disposal and more opportunities to serve than we've ever had before. I think it's up to us, at Volunteers of America, to become experts in treating and dealing with moral injury. No organization has captured or adopted this cause or taken on this clinical niche. Moral injury is at the core of most of those we serve and is certainly the root of the most severe suffering we see. Addressing moral injury head on is a fit with our faith. It's a fit with our history. It's a fit with our family. It's a fit with our future.

Let's tackle this. Let's go deep into this. I don't have the answers, so let's seek out the answers together. Let's do the research. Let's seek the funding. Let's ask God to help us. Let's go where no other organization has gone. Let's become the very best in our country at dealing with moral injury and repairing the deep damage it does to the soul. ★

MIKE KING *is president and CEO of Volunteers of America.*

"It wasn't until
I heard other
caregivers tell
their stories that
I realized we all
suffer from the
same moral injury."

RETURNING TO LIFE

RITA NAKASHIMA BROCK

On an azure afternoon in October 2012, I drove across the San Rafael Bridge that straddles the glittering water of the San Francisco Bay. I parked my car beside the looming, pale walls of San Quentin State Prison and walked up the hill to the entrance dressed in a clergy collar and Johnny Cash black.

At the check-in area I met Susan Shannon, a Tibetan Buddhist graduate student I knew at Starr King School for the Ministry in Berkeley. Susan and I were accompanied into the prison by a retired US Marine Corps Colonel and Vietnam War veteran named "Sunny," and a Dutch psychologist, Jacques Verduin, who founded and directs a nonprofit called Insight-Out, which teaches mindfulness and inner transformation in California prisons. Jacques taught trauma recovery in San Quentin for nearly two decades and started a yearlong program for inmates called GRIP (Guiding Rage into Power), which teaches emotional intelligence, victim impact awareness, and nonviolence practices.

Susan was working with Jacques and knew of my research on moral injury in veterans. She asked me if I wanted to speak to a new group of military veterans about it, and I said, "Yes, absolutely." After being cleared to enter, we made our way through the complex gauntlet of gates and down a long sidewalk through the grounds to one of the buildings.

One of the graduates of the GRIP program was Ron Self, a Marine Corps combat veteran who had secretly and unsuccessfully tried to hang himself in his cell. The rope he made broke, and he later came to in his cell surprised to be alive. Ron realized veterans needed a program of their own, but as an inmate, he could not start a group. Jacques sponsored Ron's effort through his teacher status, and the Veterans Healing Veterans from the Inside Out (VHV) program was launched. My visit, the first of three over eight months, was during VHV's first session.

As Jacques, Susan, Sunny, and I walked to the meeting room, I learned that the men in the VHV group were mostly Vietnam-era veterans, with a few from Desert Storm, and only about half had been in combat. They told me Ron was a Marine Corps special ops veteran who served from 1987 to 1996 and had a reputation in prison for being so lethal that no one bothered him.

We found the twenty men in prison blues waiting for us. Ron greeted us as we arrived. He was about six-feet tall and powerfully built, with sandy-brown hair, glasses, and a poised, self-possessed intelligence. Ron called the group to order and had everyone sit in a circle of chairs. After some preliminaries, Jacques introduced me, and I explained what I knew about moral injury.

I began by telling them about an article written by a group of U.S. Department of Veterans Affairs clinicians in 2009 that distinguished moral injury from post-traumatic stress disorder (PTSD). The clinicians described moral injury as a deeper, longer-lasting form of suffering that the VA had not been treating. Unlike PTSD, moral injury is not based in terror, and what works for PTSD may not work for moral injury, so it remained untreated.

Moral injury is an affliction of moral conscience, a negative judgment we pass on ourselves in response to violating our core moral values or to being contaminated by exposure to evil. It can lead us to feel unforgiveable for something we did, failed to do, witnessed, or endured, and it can cause us to conclude we are no longer good and decent persons. Such judgments fuel a host of moral emotions, such as guilt, shame, grief, remorse, disgust, and outrage; and when we lose meaning or faith, we also lose our ability to trust our world, others, and even ourselves. We become divided against ourselves.

Joining the military involves a profound internal change in many core values, changes that are annealed by repeated drills and the pressures of war. I did not need to tell those veterans that military training requires learning to inflict violence more efficiently and better than one's enemies or that, in the context of the military, exhibiting aggression in the face of danger is a mark of character. Veterans understand that the courage to fight and serve others is based on unit bonding, which makes combatants willing to die to save others. Their bonds of love can be so deep that they constitute the closest relationships in a young enlistee's life. Losing a friend in battle is like losing a soul mate—the deep love of a lifetime—and the losses of war are riddled with intense grief and, often, with survivor guilt. However, what even military veterans do not consider is that such bonds can render ordinary civilian relationships untrustworthy, transactional, and shallow by comparison.

Military values that veterans have learned cannot simply be set aside like an old uniform after their military service is over, even for those who never serve in combat. People can be so changed by military service that they cannot relate to the people they were before or to the families and friends who love them. The sorrow and pain veterans carry can often erupt as anger, and they end up pushing people away because they no longer trust.

For veterans with moral injury, the shift back to civilian society and values can become impossible because their moral conscience traps them in solitary mistrust and self-punishing agony. They may have lost their best friends in their unit or feel ashamed of things they did or failed to stop. They can feel so hollowed out, numb, and despairing that they cannot find their way back from emotional isolation and end up living painfully dislocated from ordinary life and relationships. They can be angry with their government, military authorities, even God. They may believe that God hates them or conclude that God does not exist. Because moral emotions such as shame, grief, guilt, and outrage are so painful, moral injury can be pushed down and carried for years, even decades, as silent, hidden suffering. Unable to go back to who they were before the military or see a way out of the pain they carry, some veterans give up or lash out in fury.

The men I met that October day listened carefully to me and asked excellent and perceptive questions. Jacques asked them if anything I said related to their life experience. Some of the men spoke of their feelings that the military had turned them into killers, and they were angry about it. One of the men who served in Vietnam said he did not return

"Moral injury is an affliction of moral conscience, a negative judgment we pass on ourselves in response to violating our core moral values or being contaminated by exposure to evil."

with "any of that PTSD stuff." He thought he was fine, but upon reflection he realized he was not. Even though he had always planned on becoming a Christian Pentecostal minister, he returned home from Vietnam an atheist and never went back to church. He never considered his rejection of faith as being related to his war experience.

As the men told harrowing stories of Vietnam, I began to think about what my own father might have experienced as a field station medic. He served two tours while I was finishing high school, and he returned a different person. He was cold, controlling, and distant. We fought a lot, and we remained estranged until he died eight years after his return home. I felt something deep inside me shift as I listened to those men talk about their experiences. The weight of the terrible details about that war began to sink in. I had never connected what happened between my father and me to the war, and as I realized how much he'd changed, I saw the impact of moral injury on my own life.

After the group adjourned for dinner, Ron lingered to talk to Jacques and me.

"This moral injury idea, I'm going to have to think about it some more," he said. After pausing a moment, he continued: "I was team leader of a special ops unit, and we completed 127 successful missions."

"I had heard you were special ops," I affirmed.

He took a deep breath.

"In our 128th mission, I lost my entire unit, including my cousin."

I took this information in for a moment, and because it was time for him to leave I could only think to say, "I'm sorry that happened to you."

"Yeah," he said softly, as something in his eyes changed. "This moral injury idea, it's important."

As we walked back to our cars, Jacques thanked me for coming and asked if I noticed something shift in Ron when he spoke to us after the meeting.

"Yes," I said. "It was subtle, but his leader persona opened a little."

Jacques had sensed it as well.

When I returned for a second visit to San Quentin in mid-December to see if our discussion of moral injury had been helpful, the group was excited to tell me that it was, in fact, the most helpful concept they had ever encountered in trying to understand their lives. Ron had started taking a prison English course that gave him access to research. He found papers on moral injury, which he read and shared with the group. We went around the circle so each of the men could share an insight that learning about moral injury had given him.

The men had discovered war and prison were very similar. Both, they said: created a total authoritarian environment that controls every aspect of life; involved sanctioned violence in life or death contexts; inflicted a high penalty for trying to leave; and offered no process to help with a transition back to ordinary life.

The biggest surprise came from Sunny, the retired Marine Corps colonel. When his turn came, he said he had not believed in such a thing as moral injury. He thought I was just giving the men excuses and a way to complain. But as he watched what happened every week in the veterans group, he said he changed his mind. He explained the concept of moral injury to a VA medical doctor who works with veterans in prisons, and the doctor told Sunny it "was the most important thing he had learned to help him treat veterans."

Sunny looked directly at me and said, "I was rude to you, and I apologize." And as he escorted me out of the prison later he confessed that he had come to think differently about his Vietnam War experience.

"I realized I have been really angry at my government," he said, "for dishonoring the military by putting us in a war they thought was unwinnable and never giving us enough support to win it."

> "When I returned...the group was excited to tell me that it was, in fact, the most helpful concept they had ever encountered in trying to understand their lives."

For recovery to happen people must speak about their moral injury, but they cannot share their deepest pain and humiliations without being able to trust the listener to receive the full truth of their experience without judgment or opinions. To share inner anguish, we need the empathetic, openhearted attention of listening friends. We need friends who take the time to hear us so we can tell the stories of what destroyed our moral universe and find ways to create a meaningful system that can enable us to integrate our trauma. Veterans Healing Veterans makes recovery from moral injury possible for those in prison because everyone involved shares a common military culture and understands each other's experiences.

When it was my turn to speak at our second meeting, I thanked the veterans for sharing their stories of moral injury. To be told another's story of pain and struggle is, I believe, a great gift of a person's trust and spirit, a gift to be respected and honored with our own honest vulnerability. I explained that they helped me feel compassion for a father I had been estranged from for more than forty years. Every Christmas, I bought poinsettia flowers at my church for people who meant a lot to me, but I had never bought one for my father. For Christmas 2012, thanks to this group of veterans, I bought a poinsettia for my father and, after forty years of a hardened heart, I started to miss him and truly grieve his passing.

My third and final visit to the prison was five months later, when the veterans met as a group for the last time. A couple of them were getting paroled, the rest were becoming facilitators for the next VHV cycle.

In a 2016 TedxSanQuentin talk, "How to End Veteran Suicide," Ron shared the story of his secret, failed suicide attempt, which took place in his prison cell in November 2011. He spoke poignantly of his love for the men he had lost in combat and eloquently of the need for a better process for people leaving the military. His solution is Boot Camp Out, a training for civilian life as ritualized and intense as boot camp in. Ron was released on parole in November 2017, and he still leads VHV but wants to make Boot Camp Out his next big project.

Through the willingness of veterans to speak of the horrors of combat, the moral anguish of war, and the searing losses of their deepest friends, they show us how many trauma survivors can experience moral injury. Without the love of friends, social support, and adequate time to overcome the pain of trauma, survivors may self-destruct slowly through addictions, overwork, failed relationships, despair, and homelessness. Some reach the end of their ability to cope and die by their own hands.

"To share inner anguish, we need the empathetic, openhearted attention of listening friends."

While moral injury experiences can never be forgotten, recovery happens via trustworthy relationships. As sharing unfolds over time with friends, the pain of moral injury can cease to dominate and destroy a life. Many veterans also seek to be of service to others and to make a difference for good, which enables them to experience a sense of worth and value. As moral injury is placed in perspective with the building of a new life, those who recover can begin to feel compassion for themselves and for others.

Moral injury is not a disorder with a clear diagnosis or symptom profile. It is a normal response to moral failure that can happen to any human being with a conscience and capacity for love and empathy. It's a dimension of human suffering familiar to all religious and humanist traditions.

Our suffering is testimony to the soul's non-negotiable requirements for meaning and connection. The anguish of moral injury reveals, paradoxically, what it hides: the indestructibility of conscience and our profound need for love. These elements of our humanity can be exhumed from beneath the outrage, distrust, shame, remorse, guilt, and despair that accompany our moral failures. The exhumation process is the beginning of our healing and restoring us to our world. I think of it as resurrection and the start of a hard-earned wisdom that is a gift to us all.

When I first encountered the concept of moral injury in late 2009, I could not have anticipated how much it would change my own life as the daughter of a combat veteran. While I have had a successful career as a feminist theologian and professor, moral injury has closed a circle in my life that needed closing. It has healed a very old wound and changed me more than any other work of my life, and it has brought me back to some the spiritual practices of the Buddhism that formed me for the first six years of my life in Japan.

I had thought I would retire someday as a senior professor, but instead I find myself living into a new chapter outside the world of academe, returning to old aspects of my life long buried. With my new position at Volunteers of America, I have an opportunity to join, through hands-on work, the intellectual capital I have accumulated with the deepest impulses of my heart to heal the brokenhearted from wounds I know myself. It's work I never imagined doing and work that feels exactly right. ★

REV. RITA NAKASHIMA BROCK, PhD, *is senior vice president, moral injury, for Volunteers of America.*

> "The anguish of moral injury reveals, paradoxically, what it hides: the indestructibility of conscience and our profound need for love."

HEALING FROM MORAL INJURY

JONATHAN SHERIN

Volunteers of America, a faith-based human services provider, is committed to uplifting the nation's most vulnerable populations. It accepts this mission of service to others as a calling it embraces, a charge it honors, and a blessing for which it is thankful. With this ethos in place since being founded in 1896, Volunteers of America recognizes that the common thread and binding feature of those it serves is exposure to trauma.

But just as people differ and responses to trauma vary, trauma itself comes in many shapes, sizes, and doses. From the trauma of fetal exposure to alcohol, drug, or cigarette smoke to the trauma of poverty, abuse at home or work, loss, excess, war and natural disaster—trauma has found, and always will find, its way into human lives.

When traumas affect us emotionally, physically, and intellectually as individuals or affect our families and social lives, it is usually apparent. Less conspicuous, however, are the signs of traumas that disrupt our belief systems and impact us morally.

These latter disruptions, resulting from core ethical transgressions and broken codes of behavior, can generate unresolvable questions about life's meaning and our place in the world, thereby disturbing our sense of values, good and bad.

Regardless of any relationship to religion or faith, our constructs of belief—in self, love, science, or higher power—author our personal narratives, give us meaning in the world, drive our affiliation with others, underlie our purpose in life, and define our morality.

As such, injuries that are the result of disturbances in belief systems can be crippling and render the human experience intolerable. Our innate resilience, coping mechanisms, and means of access to resources for support can mitigate the impact of trauma, but we are all susceptible to insults that undermine our beliefs.

Given that beliefs are roadmaps for navigating the human experience, and their destruction in the hands of trauma can be devastating, we must retain and exercise our ability to repair them.

Repair, which involves rebuilding belief systems that incorporate the past, understand the present, and position for the future anew, ultimately relies upon the establishment of neural circuit dynamics that support new psychological structures.

With psychopharmacological approaches that set the table for neural flexibility, the incorporation of updated and healthy personal narratives through therapies such as adaptive disclosure, and opportunities to reestablish belonging and purpose in life through service to others, healing is possible.

When our sense of meaning is damaged, and when our narrative becomes inadequate in a way that challenges our own organismal integrity, morality is on the chopping block and repair is required to resume the journey.

As sentient beings, we must accept our belief systems as basic constructs that provide roadmaps for understanding everyday life. As such, we can accept that these constructs, like our brains, are not set in concrete, and we can take advantage of the fact that they avail themselves to construction and destruction every day and use their plasticity to heal the moral injuries we endure. ★

JONATHAN E. SHERIN, M.D., PH.D., *is the director of the Los Angeles County Department of Mental Health.*

> "But just as people differ and responses to trauma vary, trauma itself comes in many shapes, sizes, and doses."

A SENSE OF PLACE

HARRY QUIETT

On the opening day of The Children's Garden, a Volunteers of America Carolinas daycare program for homeless children, the staff welcomed the children and showed them around the facility. Each child found a large cube with their name on it to store their belongings. Later in the day, the staff noticed several children were missing. They searched everywhere only to find the children curled up asleep inside their cubes. When asked why they were in their cubes, all the children responded: "You said it was my place."

There is something that defies description within the human spirit—it's what we call the "soul." It is fueled by that resilient part of every person, which allows him or her to move forward each day. One word we often associate with this is "hope." While we can find many descriptions of what hope looks like or means to an individual, we do not know how to create it. For hope, like life, seems to be a part of the magic of existence that the soul must discover on its own.

Moral injury is a term we now use to define the result of our soul being damaged. It's what remains when hope has fled and taken with it our sense of self and place—the things that makes us feel worthy of inclusion in the human family and our own community.

Religions all around the world seek to enlighten and support individuals in their soul's journey toward "being." However, "being" is a state of existence into which we enter, not one that we can buy or one for which there is a defined path. It is the journey of the soul.

Thus, the very essence of who we are as individuals is beyond rational comprehension. This is what makes moral injury so difficult. The conditions of moral injury are a step beyond clinical analysis; it is the injury not of the mind or body, but the soul.

Dr. Rita Brock brought this concept to the attention of the faith community by bringing faith and psychological disciplines together in her book, *Soul Repair*. Her work focuses on the military and veteran communities where severe trauma drives a high suicide rate.

Volunteers of America has been addressing human needs and trauma for more than 120 years. It has long been our conviction that we must serve the whole person— body, mind, and spirit—in order to achieve our mission of "reaching and uplifting all people and bringing them to the active service of God." Addressing severe trauma, and giving it a name, helps us give our efforts a more defined shape as we work more strategically with those we serve. We want to help people understand their own worth and give them the opportunity to find paths to repair often badly damaged souls.

> "There is something that defies description within the human spirit—it's what we call the "soul."

As an organization based in faith but dedicated to principles of social work's highest standards, we see the effect of moral injury every day. From veterans to abused children to those in the grips of addiction and poverty, the struggle for place and self-understanding underlies the adversity. After a life spent in the ecclesiastical and nonprofit worlds, I have become convinced that we must close the gap between the approaches of faith and secular society. The limits of the secular world are expanded by faith into the places beyond language and reason where mythos and logos are experienced and understood.

The term "moral injury" applies to many individuals who have endured suffering to the point that their spirit is broken. In some cases, their spirit may have never been able to fully develop. The damaging effects of poverty are well documented. A lack of economic security leads to instability, which can lead individuals to behave or act in ways that starkly contrast the moral values of our culture as well as the individual's own upbringing. Victims of poverty are sometimes led into a life of crime, which they know is wrong, but survival is a greater instinct than cultural mores. In fact, a subculture can develop in which "right" might be acknowledged as an ideal but is unrelated to present circumstances.

Two symptoms of moral injury are guilt and shame. If not understood and dealt with, these emotions can lead to anger and, ultimately, a disassociation with reality or a total loss of a sense of place.

The role of every faith community is to provide that sense of "place" where an individual can feel like a viable and valuable member of the human race. It is within that community that individuals can develop their moral compass, take a measure of their self-esteem, and feel acknowledged. As a faith-based human service movement, Volunteers of America seeks to help every individual beyond food, shelter, and material support to find that place.

Two things drive us into community—the natural human instinct for community, and suffering. Charity can address the physical suffering with clothing, food, and shelter. But healing the suffering of the soul requires the presence of God. In the Christian tradition, we understand that presence as Grace.

The theological purpose of Church is to perpetuate the faith. The purpose of faith is to nurture and heal the soul. "Church" is not a structure, it is a group of individuals who have responded to the good news of Grace and Love to reconcile a creation that has mired itself in alienation, misery, and hopelessness.

Christians and other faith communities have readily answered the call to assist those in need. Job placement, clothing drives, and much more have helped fuel the charities of the nonprofit world, but they have not always understood the complexities of the spiritual needs.

In an abundance of joy at the idea of God's grace, our emphasis has been on "overcoming." In Christian theology, death was the first and most vital obstacle to be overcome; resurrection led to a theology of "overcoming," which extended to all problems.

> "Moral injury is the injury not of the mind or body, but the soul."

However, with the development of psychology, theologians learned that the answers are more complex than simply "accepting Jesus." Some trauma cannot be simply overcome; it must be lived through and its presence may never completely go away. Psychology's grasp of this reality developed into a competition with faith. As a result, secularism has grown dramatically over the last century as psychology engages trauma without the judgment that often accompanies religious counseling; it has grasped the undefinable nature of the struggle of the soul. Pastoral care has emerged as a discipline that seeks to bridge the gap and understand the plight of the suffering soul.

Likewise, there has often been tension between professional social work and ministry. While they have similar objectives, the social worker is more in touch with the complexities of the trauma that brings an individual to ask for assistance. The Christian Church, at least in the lay theology of most members, likes simple answers. Actions, ideas, and policies are either "right" or "wrong" based on religious convictions. Unfortunately, those convictions are frequently poorly informed theologically. After all, has not the "Church Triumphant" put suffering behind it in the sacrifice of Jesus?

While all moral injury is suffering, not all suffering is moral injury. There is a spectrum from moral stress to moral injury, which is not always easily defined. Caregivers are specifically subject to moral stress and sometimes even moral injury. Many of the issues they face in determining the best care and providing adequate attention can evolve into deep moral conflicts. Caregiving in a situation such as Alzheimer's, when a loved one may not only lose memory but also lose touch with current reality, weighs heavily on the caregiver. Under those circumstances, moral stress in inevitable.

New and continuing research on moral injury and avenues to treatment can help pastoral care faith communities begin to understand and address the complex issue of moral injury/spiritual trauma. This research can begin to assist faith communities to accomplish their already defined mission: helping all souls achieve their full potential in God's creation.

As Volunteers of America continues "to reach and uplift all people and bring them to the active knowledge of God," we continue to attempt to understand and address the intense suffering that defies simple solutions. As we offer care, we want to provide all people with the opportunity that our founders staked out in 1896: a chance for wholeness and a place in the Kingdom of God. While we do this from a Christian

> "The role of every faith community is to provide that 'place' where an individual can feel like a viable and valuable member of the human race."

perspective, God does not exclude anyone from grace. Our challenge is to awaken each individual's own faith walk to wherever place that journey may lead them.

Understanding and addressing moral injury may be a means to addressing the divide between psychology and religion. We may finally come to realize that they are different sides of one coin and helping severely traumatized individuals will require assistance from both. An individual may have issues that psychology can address, but the faith community must embrace its role in the mysteries of existence that only faith can perceive. Our role as a Church is to welcome each person into community and confirm that he or she is an individual of worth, is a member of the human family, and someone who has a right to a place to call their own. ★

REV. HARRY QUIETT *is vice president, ministry development, for Volunteers of America.*

"Some trauma cannot be simply overcome; it must be lived through and its presence may never completely go away."

*Recovery from
moral injury requires
telling one's story
and being heard.*

REDISCOVERING MY SOUL

AL PERATT, SR.

It's 1988, I'm 37-years-old, and I'm sitting in my prison cell wondering why I'm even here.

I started a journal at the recommendation of my teacher at Chino State Prison in Chino, California. He encouraged me to look at my life to figure out who I am and where I came from, and to examine significant events that led me from San Diego, California to a maximum security prison in Sioux Falls, South Dakota.

I think back to when I first started my prison time, and the prison psychiatrist asked me if I wanted to hear his diagnosis. I wanted the drugs he had, so I said, "Sure!" When he replied that he thought I could have very easily been a serial killer, I said: "I'm just a drug dealer, but don't give me any ideas, Doc!" And, by the way, thanks for my drugs!

But he was right. I could have very easily ended up much worse than I was.

Since then, I have received treatment for post-traumatic stress disorder through the Veterans Administration and am now an ordained minister within the Southern Baptist Convention and Volunteers of America, so the subject of moral injury intrigued me.

See, earlier in life, my two brothers, older sister and I were sent to foster homes. My father was in the military—U.S. Navy, Chief Engine Room Officer, WWII veteran, submariner. My mother wasn't around.

After the foster homes, we moved back with our father into a blended home, where our stepmother was a dominant and strict woman who was not afraid of giving the belt. At some point, she and my father were "saved" in a Southern Baptist Church. Afterward, in the name of Jesus, I was "corrected" many times.

I was put in a cold shower for wetting the bed and had to wear a sandwich-board sign announcing my accident to all my schoolmates. I endured belt beatings and long periods of "restriction" in my room. And I was the "Yes, Sir; No, Ma'am; Please and Thank You" poster child. If not, I was slapped or got the belt.

After getting in trouble for skipping a Youth for Christ meeting to attend a high school dance, I was required to have a sit down with the leader of the young men's group at our church; he was my dad's best friend. With a picture of Jesus on the wall and a cold pop in my hand, we sat in the choir room and he asked me if I knew why I got in trouble while he molested me. That incident determined my outlook on life: no one can be trusted.

In her book, *Soul Repair*, author Rita Nakashima Brock states, "In experiencing a moral conflict, soldiers may judge themselves as worthless; they may decide no one can be trusted and isolate themselves from others; and they may abandon the values and beliefs that gave their lives meaning and guided their moral choices."

> "By the time I graduated from high school, I had already lived a few lifetimes."

By the time I graduated from high school, I had already lived a few lifetimes.

But they weren't all bad times. We had swimming pool parties, and beach trips, went to Disneyland, and played sports. But the undercurrent was that we never knew the climate at home at any given time. It could get downright dark at the drop of a dime.

As a young adult, I started cutting myself or making my lips bleed to make it look like I had gotten into fights. I didn't realize at that time that my confusion and low self-esteem was leading me down a path of moral value abandonment.

I was kicked out of college for drinking on campus. I wanted to do well, but for some reason would end up testing the system through drugs and alcohol. Eventually, I joined the military where I was a legal clerk during the day and the top hashish dealer at night.

Drugs and alcohol became my escape. After I left the military, I met my wife and discovered she, too, had a background filled with moral injury. We felt comfortable with each other.

In *Soul Repair*, a quote from General G.C. Marshall resonates with me: "The soldier's heart, the soldier's spirit, the soldier's soul are everything." My soul has been fractured most of my life. I was more comfortable being around the depressed, oppressed, addicted, and convicted as they never judged me for the way I led my life.

I left Los Angeles and ended up in San Diego where I fought fires in the San Diego Fire Camps and eventually got busted for smuggling heroin. I received a five-to-life sentence, which I served in Chino State Prison.

My soul was lost. I was slowly drifting away and accepting that the life I was destined to live was one of jails, institutions, and, eventually, death. I didn't foresee living to 30 years old.

After prison, I became a heroin addict for almost eight years. My wife at the time had a significant methamphetamine habit. She and I were slowly drifting away. After we had a particularly violent argument, my son and I moved to South Dakota where I thought I could get away from drugs and alcohol. But my wife and I ended up back together, and we started one of the biggest Meth rings that ever existed in the Black Hills of South Dakota.

Everything came crashing down with a narcotics bust, and I was sent to the state penitentiary in Sioux Falls, South Dakota for a ten-year sentence. My wife was pregnant with our daughter, and my son was too young to understand what was going on. It was a dark, spiritual time in our lives.

After a year in prison, I was getting ready to do a drug treatment program and talking like I wanted to change my life. But as the Apostle Paul says, "Another law is waging war against the law of my mind." See, I was saying I wanted to change, but it was just talk. God has ways of opening our eyes when we can't see the truth for what it is.

I like the way *Soul Repair* explains Spiritual Fitness: "Strengthening a set of beliefs, principles or values that sustain a person beyond family, institutional, and societal sources of strength."

I needed something more powerful than drugs to set my moral compass. I didn't trust most people, but I decided to make a commitment to God that wherever he led me I would tell the truth about my life in addiction and conviction. He is faithful when we deliver our lives to his will.

I completed a business degree and paralegal degree while in prison. Upon my release, I was allowed to go to work, 12-step meetings, and church. I did just that, and I did it a lot.

I spent 15 years with Hutchinson Technologies, Inc., a computer-based company where I eventually became a supervisor. When the company moved, I ended up with Volunteers of America, Dakotas as their Chaplain. I've been with Volunteers of America for more than nine years.

"My soul has been fractured most of my life."

My church licensed me to preach the gospel in the local county jail where the sheriff allowed me to lead a Bible study. I was also asked by one of the local treatment centers to hear the 5th step of the 12-step program. I eventually heard more than 8,000 5th steps in nearly 20 years at that treatment center. I still hear a few, but I mostly give lectures on changing our spirituality to become productive members of society. I was even asked to be a volunteer chaplain by a warden that used to see me locked up.

In 2011, after 14-and-a-half years of waiting to hear whether the president of the United States would grant me a pardon, I received one of the nine given out that year by President Barack Obama. What a phone call that was, and what a celebration I had with my beautiful bride, Teresa. She has been with me on this crazy journey for 43 years.

I was diagnosed with tongue cancer in 2012 and endured seven weeks straight of radiation and chemotherapy. I even went into a coma for more than a month and died once. My survival is another example of God wanting to give me more time to tell people the truth about the dark side of our moral world and how we can come out the other side into the light. In 2016, Volunteers of America named me the Leader of Ministry for its affiliates. It was an honor.

When I look back at my life, I see a man that has been shot, stabbed, run over by a truck, walks with a limp and has arthritis all over. But my physical injuries are nothing compared to the spiritual injuries I've endured. Being morally injured and morally injuring others are things I'll have to live with for the rest of my life.

Through helping others, I have found that faith can move mountains. I also know that I can count on God to send me someone every day who needs to hear stories of hope and confirmation that there is light at the end of the tunnel.

The sooner we crawl out of our past moral injuries into the light of redemption, the sooner our stories of salvation can be used to help others.

Be blessed my brothers in arms and children of God! ★

PASTOR AL PERATT *is the chaplain for Volunteers of America, Dakotas.*

> "Through helping others, I have found that faith can move mountains."

"God has ways of opening our eyes when we can't see the truth for what it is."

SHARING TRUTH & HEALING WOUNDS

ANGELA ARCOS

The first time my fiancée attacked me I was pregnant with our son.

He put his hands around my neck and squeezed to the moment before blackout. He smacked my head against a cement wall. He ripped up clothing and stomped on a laptop. He was drunk.

The next morning I felt the welts on my head, tender and pulsing. I touched the bruises on my neck. I knew I had to run. I had to get away. *This is the first incident from which all the other incidents will be born*, I thought.

A week later we got married.

He convinced me it would never happen again, and I convinced myself I had to believe him. He'd been emotionally manipulative and abusive for years, but, because that's a sneakier form of abuse, I hadn't been able to identify and label it. I knew something was wrong. I was becoming angrier. I began screaming when I was upset. I thought I was crazy.

I felt so much shame the morning after the first beating. Suffering the cruelty of words and enduring the psychological control, I felt like a covered pot of macaroni boiling away, the white froth nearing the top and threatening to spill out. The violent assault was like taking the lid off—I finally felt release. The physicality allowed the turmoil inside me to reduce to a simmer. I had something to hold onto now. Maybe I wasn't crazy. There was an odd safety in that knowledge. Almost satisfaction.

My stomach turns when I confront the dark reality: the knots on my head were both painful and a pleasure. The bruises were visual proof of what my heart felt. That was the first frayed edge in the unraveling of what I knew to be right and true. I compromised my fragile and beautiful humanity for a person who neither saw nor cared for my fragility and beauty. I knew it was wrong to stay, but I did.

Nobody ever imagines or fantasizes about being in an abusive relationship. I never thought it was possible for someone like me. I'd seen movies and heard stories of other women and always thought, *how sad for them. I am so much stronger than that. I would never let someone treat me that way.* When I suddenly became that woman and allowed a person—my husband—to treat me that way, I felt partially at fault. *I must be broken and ugly inside,* I thought. *I am bringing this on myself. If I could just be happier. Or better at everything.*

Slowly, I began to fade. I lost weight. My joints ached. I was ill most days. I didn't know myself anymore. My mind was a clouded, confusing place. Where I once held convictions and ideals that made me feel confident, I became unsure. The woman I once was and the woman I hoped to become were lost like a pair of cheap sunglasses. They slipped away, and I was left raw and exposed, unrecognizable to myself.

> "The bruises were visual proof of what my heart felt."

It was my birthday and an argument escalated out of control. This time he wasn't drunk. But this time I participated. As if a hidden rage was exposed, I slapped back and screamed. One moment I tried to calm us both down, the next I was egging him on. I wanted another a bruise. Of course, what I really wanted was a loving husband and a safe relationship. Instead, a physical marking became a badge I could wear to show my husband what kind of hurt he was causing me. As if a bruise could convey the despair I carried inside.

Over time I learned that if I could "out crazy" him I could sometimes prevent a situation from escalating. If I noticed he was nearing his nuclear detonation button, I would scream or slap first. I knew if I became a cyclone of shrieking and tears it would distract him and force him to quiet me down. It felt disgusting to think and act that way, but I truly thought I was the commander of that manipulation. Of course, I wasn't. It was just another way he pulled my strings and kept me in an upside-down state of desperation. He was the manipulator. I was helpless. I was so out of control of my own life that it seemed I had only two choices: quiet victim or emotionally unstable tornado.

Finally, one evening during a routine attack of verbal abuse, I tried to commit suicide. I'm humiliated to admit it. I can barely type these words without backspacing. I would like to delete this from memory. But I cannot. I wanted to die. I also wanted my husband to really *know*, to *understand* the unbearable pain he caused me. My son was sleeping in his crib, and I didn't think about him. I did not consider his life or his needs.

We all develop a list of things we would never do. As we grow and go through life, we decide who we are and what we stand for. Our identities are, in part, described by a code of ethics we write for ourselves. As my personal code was compromised over and over, I felt so far away from myself that death often seemed the only way out. I was wandering in a thick fog, my eyes seeing nothing but bleakness, my lungs breathing nothing but thick guilt and despair.

I will remember the things my son saw and his cries as he clung to my legs. I can sink deep into memories of being so wrapped up in my own torment and panic that I would forget my child was asleep and needed me to be stable and nurturing when he woke. When I try to reconcile the choices I made with the actions or inactions I am guilty of, it leaves me full of shame.

My husband created a fog and locked me in it like a prisoner. But five months after my suicide attempt, while frayed, damaged, and weak, I took my son and left.

What I struggle with now is catching glimpses of my husband's temper in myself. Was it always there, lurking and waiting for an appropriate trigger? Was it behavior learned as a way to communicate with my partner? Or am I just a single mother who occasionally loses her patience?

I'm not sure, but the answer doesn't really matter. The truth is that the temper is there and I have to fight against it almost every day. I am determined to not repeat the cycle, and I keep trying to be better than yesterday. Sometimes I fail. But I keep trying.

The best prescription I have for healing these wounds is a combination of two things: radical empathy and truth.

I begin by extending an empathetic hand to myself. I remind myself that I am alone now and while not unpleasant, it is difficult. I tell myself that I love myself and that what I am feeling is understandable, but I need to be bigger than my emotions. I must regain the strength and beauty of my soul by rebuilding with each and every moment of choice. And I choose light and love, patience and empathy.

Then I show empathy for my son. By validating and respecting him, I can do my part to see that he grows into a man without a furnace of rage within his heart. He will learn from me what it looks like to make mistakes, to instantly regret them and to soften your heart, apologize, talk about it, and repair. He is already utilizing the deep-breathing method I employ when I feel the need to yell welling up.

In my quiet reflections I offer empathy to my ex-husband. Because he could pose a threat to our new and peaceful life, I do not dialogue this with him. Only in my heart do I allow myself to understand him and see him as a small child who was not given patience and guidance. I allow myself to see parts of me in him and to know that we are all products of our story. While that does not release us from responsibility, it does provide an opportunity for empathy. I can love the small child he once was, just like the son I have now. I can love the little girl that I once was and still carry around inside me. With that love and empathy, I can move forward with a little less anger.

Then comes the truth. That is my purpose here. To share my truth in all its unpleasantness, with honesty and bravery, is like a healing balm. We must talk about our ugly places. Shining light in the dark corners of our souls keeps the infectious mold of self-contempt from taking hold. ★

ANGELA ARCOS *is a blogger and freelance writer living in Arkansas.*

"As my personal code was compromised over and over, I felt so far away from myself that death often seemed the only way out."

A LIFE WITH PURPOSE

ANONYMOUS

I was born into a single-parent home to a mother who was just six months shy of her twentieth birthday and a father who wasn't around. My mother and my maternal grandparents raised me. My father took his own life when I was a toddler.

When I was a young boy, a man my mother married sexually abused me. The abuse went on for a while before my family found out, then my mom divorced him.

When I was nine, I lost my two-year-old sister in a fire. I could hear her screaming and crying. I tried to get to her but couldn't reach her through the flames, heat, and smoke. The firefighters found her in my bed. She died a couple weeks later.

I grew up working hard on farms, studying at school, playing sports, working in restaurants, going to church, and loving my family. My mom remarried a second time and started a family, and I was blessed with more siblings. After I graduated from high school, I left home, moved to a different state, and went to college. While in college, I realized I wanted to serve my country, so I joined the United States Marine Corps.

My military service was filled with good and bad times, but it gave me a sense of purpose, a sense of pride, a sense of self-respect, and sense of worth—things I hadn't felt in a long time. Helping people is in my blood.

But being helpful to people comes with its angels and its demons. My demons surfaced when I got divorced and my toddler son was moved to the other side of the country. I wasn't able to make ends meet. My soul was drained of its life. My heart was broken, and my mind was numb. And after seeing and facing death so many times in so many forms, all of this loss at once finally broke me. I was ready to embrace death.

I took my pistol and loaded it so there were "10 in the clip and one in the hole." Holding it in my right hand, I stared into the barrel and put the pistol to my head. With my finger on the trigger, I was prepared to enter eternity. The only things I felt I had to lose were all the years of pain, shame, guilt, and anger.

Then something happened. When I held the pistol to my head and closed my eyes, I envisioned the face of my sweet little boy. I *did* have something to lose. I felt the loss of not seeing him grow up, of no longer hugging him, of not being able to tell him I love him. I thought about the impact taking my life would have on him.

I took my finger off the trigger. I moved the pistol away from my head. I wept like I hadn't wept in a long time. My son saved my life.

I was able to find support through my family, my faith, my God, and my friends. They helped me work through my moral injury. I still deal with my demons, but now I am able to address them before they consume me. I joined the Army National Guard, and I currently hold a leadership role there. I am a Volunteers of America ordained minister and an original member of the Volunteers of America National Veterans Resource Squad (NVRS).

> "When I held the pistol to my head and closed my eyes, I envisioned the face of my sweet little boy."

I have suffered spiritually, emotionally, mentally, and physically, but these experiences have taught me the importance of being trusted. The training I received as part of the NVRS, and as a Volunteers of America minister, has enabled me to be trusted by my military leaders, by the soldiers, and my colleagues. It also led to me being appointed the Suicide Prevention and Assistance Training Noncommissioned Officer for more than 120 soldiers. I was also named quasi-chaplain so the soldiers can talk to me about anything and everything. And they do. I am fortunate to be where I am and to have been given a second chance.

My motivation to help others and recognize when they are hurting is—and will forever be—shaped by my experiences. But I've also found inspiration in the Charlie

"I am fortunate to be where I am and to have been given a second chance."

Chaplin film *The Great Dictator*. In the film's final scene, Chaplin's character says, "We all want to help one another. Human beings are like that. The way of life can be free and beautiful."

In 2013, my first daughter was born. Three years later, I attended my son's Little League game and saw him pitch for the first time. That same year, my second daughter was born.

I have a purpose. And man is it a great day to be alive! ★

HOPE, REDISCOVERED

BILL KEEGAN

"A small plane just crashed into the North Tower of the World Trade Center complex . . . you need to respond." With that phone call, my life's path was altered in ways I could have never imagined.

I was a Port Authority police lieutenant assigned to the Special Operations Division, a unit specifically designed to respond to major incidents. After I received that phone call on September 11, 2001, I raced up a closed New Jersey turnpike, in and out of the slower moving military trucks and ambulances. A second plane had struck the South Tower and both towers lay in ruins among the burning, yet still-standing, buildings in the complex. The car radio kept delivering gut-wrenching blasts; the news grew grimmer, and I tried to concentrate on my training and the tasks that would lie ahead.

My mind kept wandering back to February 26, 1993—the first World Trade Center bombing. I lived much closer to New York City then, and, unlike this day, I arrived at the World Trade Center quickly enough to extract elementary school kids from a stalled elevator on the 43rd floor. Had I not been at the hospital with my daughter on the morning of September 11, I would have been in the towers conducting the evacuation. Like many of my colleagues, I may not have survived.

As I turned east toward the Hudson River, I saw smoke wafting south from the scarred skyline of New York City. To my left stood the green steeple of my church, where I once served as an altar boy and member of the choir, and where my moral compass was constructed with a strong magnetic north—a belief system based on the goodness of man. What I was about to experience would challenge all that I held sacred and true.

I arrived at the Port Authority Police Department command vehicle around 2 p.m., thirsty for information, ready to formulate plans, eager to help. I stood on the corner of North Moore and West Street staring south at the space where the crown jewels of New York City once stood; now they were just ruins, reminiscent of the Coliseum in Rome or Hamburg, Germany, following World War ll.

A PAPD sergeant was briefing me on the conditions just a few blocks away. He was very methodical and business-like, just as we were trained. I looked into the faces covered in white concrete powder, their eyes in a trance-like stare as they walked aimlessly back and forth. I remember how surreal the report seemed, how the rat-tat-tat cadence of the words poured from his lips. I became distracted and almost didn't notice when he said: "We have about 50 members missing."

"Hold up," I said. "What do you mean missing? Are they in the hospital, working the pile? What do you mean missing?"

"I'm sorry, boss," he replied.

"They are missing and presumed dead? No, they're probably just working, haven't checked in. They're working, maybe escorted others to the hospital."

The sergeant's lips began to quiver, and his voice shook as he blurted out: "Lieutenant, you got to see what it's like down there. They're gone. It's a mess … they're gone."

There it was: Presumed dead. Gone. The thousand-yard stares of the almost catatonic witnesses to this horror made much more sense now. This couldn't be. The neat box of "response, training, and just another job" that I tucked this incident into was completely shattered. The pain was not vicarious but real in every sense. I was standing, but I was out on my feet like a stunned boxer who keeps punching. I kept talking, not knowing what I was saying because it didn't matter—they were gone.

It didn't seem possible that such evil existed among us, that a person would have such a depraved sense of humanity that he thought it was a good thing to kill so many innocent people. I always held that good defeats evil. That mantra was drummed into me by the nuns, the priests and my parents, back from my days praying in that church. Even my black-and-white TV screen sent the unambiguous message that the "good guy" prevails …always. A small group of terrorists would change that calculus, would smash my moral compass and leave me questioning not only how God could allow this to happen but whether there is a God. How could I go on if my shaken faith had left me with no hope?

For the next eight months, I led hundreds of professionals as we tried to bring some comfort to the loved ones of those who perished in the 9/11 attacks. Our mission would ebb and flow with a range of emotions. We became very proficient in matching body parts like socks; our nights were dotted with grisly discoveries that were repulsive yet joyful. The moral incongruence of our duty was very evident, and we struggled nightly.

Ultimately, it was our commitment to comfort the loved ones who lost family that began to restore our moral direction. Just as we had to simplify our physical response to the catastrophic challenges presented by the crumbling of the towers, we also had to simplify our spiritual navigation. We could not change the loss of life, the destruction, or the grief, but we could provide some comfort to the survivors by bringing their loved ones home.

> "I was standing, but I was out on my feet like a stunned boxer who keeps punching."

We performed this horrific duty in the service of others, putting aside our own aspirations as professionals. Our vocation would fundamentally transform us. We rose from the simple gift of giving to those we did not know, to the awareness that through our altruism we would begin to rediscover our faith and, ultimately, our hope.

It was a journey that was hard traveled, with many trips and falls, but it strengthened our belief that we can overcome the darkness that some would like to spread and that light will break through even in the darkest times. Even in this crucible of horror, the loving human spirit will not only survive, it will flourish. ★

BILL KEEGAN *is president and CFO of HEART 9/11, a nonprofit disaster relief organization committed to rebuilding communities and rebuilding lives of individuals coping with disasters and related trauma, including our returning veterans.*

STORIES OF SUFFERING

A Therapist's Approach to Moral Injury

BILL GIBSON

I have the best job in the world. Every day, I get to listen as people tell me their stories. The stories are often painful for the person to tell and painful for me to hear. But they're real. They're the fabric from which we weave our lives.

People tell me stories of abuse—sexual, physical, emotional, verbal. They describe neglect and abandonment. They share stories of rape and assault and stories of combat. They tell stories of horrors committed and horrors witnessed. They tell stories of moral injury.

A patient sits in my office. He comes to me because he's wrestling with depression, anxiety, grief, or post-traumatic stress disorder. He tells me his story, and we review his history. Then I ask, "In addition to all you've described to me, I wonder if something else is going on that may be contributing to how you're feeling. Have you ever heard of moral injury?" The patient says no or gives me a puzzled shake of the head. I start to describe moral injury and what it feels like, and I see tears come to his eyes. "That's it," he says. "That's how I feel—I've never been able to put it into words."

As a therapist, these moments are sacred to me. I feel privileged to witness the birth of a person's new understanding of information about himself and his experiences that have been mysteries for years. Together, we've begun a new phase of his journey.

I've come to believe it's crucial to introduce everyone—my patients, my students, clergy, therapists, and caregivers—to the concept of moral injury. I have seen how facing moral injury and understanding what it is helps people who are suffering.

Talking about moral injury can ease the ache a veteran feels when he thinks about the dead Iraqi girl whose eyes he didn't close. Attending to her would have cost him only a few seconds, but he was too hyped up on adrenaline from combat to stop and perform this basic act of respect. Now her eyes haunt his dreams.

Addressing moral injury can help a young woman sexually abused by her father explore her shame about remaining silent. She feared if she told her mother, her father would go to jail and the family would lose everything. Understanding moral injury can help that same father finally face his shame and guilt at betraying the sacred trust of parenthood.

Learning about moral injury can help a son understand his anger at his elderly mother. She has always been demanding but now her demands are repetitive and contradictory, often nonsensical. When he ignores her or pretends he doesn't hear her, he feels guilty and ashamed because he feels like he's neglecting her. When he addresses this complicated relationship and the distress of trying to honor his parent and himself, he can ameliorate his guilt and learn how to handle the situation with less shame and greater compassion.

Understanding moral injury can help men and women in despair who are angry with God and who have lost their sense of meaning. By recognizing the complicated emotions that accompany a sense of betrayal, as well as the grief of losing one's faith in God and oneself, we can begin to rebuild our spiritual connection.

The concept of moral injury is both new and ancient. Descriptions of moral injury exist in Greek tragedies, though the term emerged in the mid-1990s. In my 25 years as a therapist, moral injury is the most exciting concept I've identified for getting to the heart of suffering. I believe it underlies much of the pain most people feel every day but few are able to articulate.

When we talk about moral injury—how it feels and the events that can cause it—we are talking about the deepest parts of ourselves. We are talking about what makes us most human and our fundamental sense of right and wrong. We are talking about our need for connection with others and our profound sense of loss when that connection ruptures.

Moral injury puts a name to something many feel. But naming something is only the first step to truly understanding it.

If you came to my office, I would talk to you about moral injury. I would tell you we needed to distinguish between what is moral injury and what isn't.

Not every bad thing that happens to us results in moral injury. Sometimes we feel moral stress, a natural tension that arises out of the friction between our values and the values of friends, family, or society. It's also important not to confuse moral injury with moral distress—the upset we feel when an external force, or something inside us, blocks us from doing what we believe is right.

But if you tell me you've done things that violate your core sense of right and wrong or that you've stood by while someone else committed morally repulsive acts, we would talk about moral injury. If you describe a powerful sense of betrayal by someone you trusted, if you talk about feeling shame, guilt, anger, and despair, we would talk about moral injury.

As a therapist, it's tempting to try to shoehorn moral injury into some diagnostic category. Human beings like to apply a quick fix, a medication, or a structured, 12-session approach to therapy that promises to make the pain go away. But moral injury doesn't fit into a neat diagnostic box. A traditional approach may reduce symptoms, but it won't get at the core of what's causing them.

I would emphasize that moral injury is not a mental illness. It may come disguised as depression or substance abuse or anger or PTSD, but it is not any of these things. I would tell you—and remind myself—moral injury is about suffering, not symptoms, and suffering is messy.

> "In my 25 years as a therapist, moral injury is the most exciting concept I've identified for getting to the heart of suffering."

Though I'm not a medical doctor, as we talk about emotional symptoms, I would ask about physical health problems. Headaches, chest pains, persistent upset stomach, trouble sleeping, loss of appetite, fatigue, malaise—these symptoms could be physical manifestations of moral injury. I would encourage you to get a thorough medical checkup, but we would also talk about how the body has a memory of its own, how it can speak of suffering deeper than words.

I would ask about your religious and spiritual history. Your moral injury may appear as a loss of faith or as an existential crisis. You may use religious or spiritual language to describe your suffering. I would ask if you've talked to a chaplain or your pastor, and, if not, if you wanted to. Whether in the form of traditional religious practice or something unique to the person, spirituality plays a valuable role in helping us understand and deal with moral injury.

We would discuss the dangers of moralism and a judgmental theology that can further damage the morally injured person. We would consider how quick and cheap forgiveness or a superficial rationalization—you were just doing your job—is no comfort at all. I'd encourage you to find a member of the clergy who is capable of traveling with you through hard country, where simplistic answers only do more harm.

Finally, I would offer that your psychiatrist, your therapist, and your religious counselor are only a part of the answer to the question your suffering poses. I would tell you that a healing community is a key ingredient in addressing your moral injury. Friends and family, a faith community, and a supportive group of people who understand what you've been through do as much good as a professional. If you didn't already have such a community, I would help you find or create one.

Many people who experience traumatic events that result in moral injury say that living through those experiences places them in a separate category. "Normal people" whose lives have never been touched by trauma or tragedy can hang onto the fantasy that the world is a kind and safe place, that other people are benevolent and helpful, and that bad things only happen to bad people. The survivors, the ones who know different because they have experienced horrific events, know better. I would ask if you feel cut off from other people, if you feel damned or like damaged goods.

Then we would talk about this false division. There is no Us and Them—there is only Us. Suffering, grief, shame, and guilt are all human emotions that everyone experiences to some degree. When we share these experiences with each other and when we hold safe space for each other, those with moral injury may find words to tell their stories. And when we share each other's stories and ease each other's suffering, we are doing sacred work.

I have the best job in the world. People tell me their stories. Together we try to understand their experiences and their suffering. Together we give each other hope. ★

WILLIAM GIBSON, PhD, *is a clinical psychologist and neuropsychologist who works in the federal government serving veterans experiencing PTSD, moral injury and related conditions. He is married to Bobbi L'Hullier (following essay).*

"...when we share each other's stories and ease each other's suffering, we are doing sacred work."

MORAL INJURY & MARRIAGE

BOBBI L'HULLIER

"My mother died when I was little, maybe five or six," William told me the first night we met. He went on to say he could not recall what she looked like and that he had no pictures of her. He and his father moved around a lot, from small town to small town in western Pennsylvania and Ohio where he grew up. Stuff got lost. Memorabilia. Photographs. Stability.

"I haven't talked to my father in almost ten years," I told him that night. "My sister and I live with our mom and help take care of her. She has Chronic Obstructive Pulmonary Disease pretty bad."

I told him about my adulterous and alcoholic father, my parents' bad divorce, and the constant worry of taking care of someone who passively wants to die, someone with a volcanic temper, someone who'd been unhappy longer than I'd been alive.

In spite of these revelations, we found a thousand ways to make each other laugh. We had a spark between us that grew from attraction to friendship to marriage. Happily ever after, and all that.

But. If you never really learn to connect deeply with other people, intimacy can become a challenge when serious issues crop up.

If your go-to emotion is anger, you have trouble expressing what you really feel while pushing other people away.

If you grew up feeling unsafe, neglected, verbally and emotionally abused, guilty, and ashamed of who you are and the people you come from, navigating the dynamics of a marriage can become a battlefield with multiple injuries.

We have gone through so much plain stress and moral stress, and even moral distress, together: three moves, a divorce, my brother's death, two new jobs, my father's unexpected return to our lives, a medical event for my mother that left her mostly bedridden, our wedding and honeymoon, my mother's death. And that was just in the first two years. Then there was another move, the death of my father's second wife, my father moving in with us, a job change, another new job, and kicking my father out of our house.

We endured many major life events together. Sometimes we were able to support one another. Sometimes we were not.

We have some protective factors: William's experience as a psychologist and his inclination to look for the best in people, and my long interest in marriage and family therapy issues and an inclination to solve problems rather than allow them to fester.

And still we hurt one another. We forgot—or did not fully understand—how our backgrounds continue to affect us. We know each other's stories. We've had countless conversations about our childhoods, about the good traits we got from our parents and families and bad traits we want to avoid. We've discussed past relationships, the lessons we gained from our losses and failures, forgiveness, and limitations on what we could forgive. We talked about big issues: death, money, careers, infidelity, loyalty, trust, happiness, depression, anxiety, procrastination, willful ignorance. We talked about guilt, pain, shame, anger, the conscious and unconscious, systems theory and Jung, minimization, and hyperbole.

But we never talked about moral injury.

When we married in 2007, neither of us had heard of moral injury. When we discovered the concept in 2013, William thought it applied mostly to veterans.

I, however, see everything through a family/relationship, systems-oriented lens and saw moral injury applying more widely. Per Jonathan Shay's definition, I

> "We endured many major life events together. Sometimes we were able to support one another. Sometimes we were not."

identified moral injury as occurring when someone in a position of authority (mom or dad) morally betrays someone for whom they are responsible (the child) in a high-stakes situation (almost total dependence on parent to meet physical, mental, emotional, and spiritual needs until able to support self). I had firsthand experience with this application. To experience moral injury, you don't have to go to a warzone if you grew up in one.

Though our perceptions differed at first, William and I both saw the benefit of identifying moral injury in people who found relief through therapeutic care yet continued to experience haunting, debilitating pain. The concept of moral injury gave us a window into why a person who seemed to be turning her life around might suddenly commit suicide—or less dramatically, might reach a stopping point in her recovery that she could not seem to overcome.

This kind of suffering requires better responses than "just get over it," or "other people have gone through worse." It also requires the willingness to understand how precipitating events, and any suffering that follows, critically affects our core identity. We spend our lives answering the question "Who am I?" to others, to ourselves, to whatever spiritual or existential system we subscribe to. When something or someone disrupts our ability to see ourselves as a good person, as someone worthy of love, kindness, support, as someone who deserves to exist, we rarely just get over it. We might keep going, we might rise again, we might achieve many and great things.

And yet. We can still carry the burdens of doubt and shame. We can go through the motions of our lives with a crippling sense of despair because of what we have done or what we have experienced. We can believe we are responsible for others' unspeakable treatment. Or we can think: I let this happen, I should have been better, acted differently, refused, interfered. If only. But I didn't, and now I am cut off from all the happy, normal people who can live their lives without this pain. Nothing can ever change it.

Moral injury is not a disease or a disorder, so we have no magic cure or quick-fix program to follow. Yet left on its own, it can distort our thinking and lead us into isolation, self-sabotage, anxiety, and apathy. We can become depressed from leaving traumatic events unaddressed while our negative feelings dismantle the life we knew and the life we see going on around us but never experience.

> "To experience moral injury, you don't have to go to a warzone if you grew up in one."

With a better understanding of moral injury, I try to imagine my husband's childhood experiences: losing his mother, which created an enormous chasm between him and the other children he encountered; having a father who loved him but who did not always know how to look out for himself or his son; the stress of being frequently uprooted by his father's sense of wanderlust and changing schools once or twice during each year; his father marrying a woman he knew his son disliked and allowing this woman to treat his son badly.

Viewing these events as a cumulative moral injury can sometimes help me see where William is especially vulnerable. His ability to recognize how his past continues to affect his future helps him communicate with greater openness. He can tell me what it felt like to grow up poor and different and afraid all the time and knows I will listen to his experiences without judgment. We can honor his father's effort to raise him without ignoring the choices his dad made that contributed to William's residual moral distress.

And William has come to understand my anger better. He understands how the anger is often the result of the anxiety or guilt I feel for not being able to make my mother's life better or that it harks back to repeated betrayals from my father's narcissistic behaviors. William doesn't understand why I refer to my parents as knife-fighters who would cut each other to pieces with their arguments, and then turn their vicious tongues onto their children. He doesn't know what it's like to be seven and have Mom wake you in the middle of the night to pack up whatever you can grab so she can leave him then end up cowering on the couch the rest of the night witnessing their battle rage on. Nor can he know what it's like to watch your mother grow weaker and more despondent then accede to her wish to not call a doctor even though you both know she is dying.

But he tries. And I try.

In the end, it doesn't matter that he holds a PhD in clinical and neuropsychology and that I have extensive training in communications. What matters is that we are both human, we love and care about one another, and we are willing to help one another find ways to suffer less.

And that's enough to keep us going. ★

BOBBI L'HUILLIER *is a writer/editor currently on the quality assurance and spotlight writing teams for a large national business consulting and education company. She is married to Bill Gibson (previous essay).*

"Moral injury is
not a disease or
a disorder, so we
have no magic
cure or quick-fix
program to follow."

ON MY WAY

CARLOS RODRIGUEZ, JR.

In 2014, I began my military medical retirement from the Army, divorced my wife of seven years, lost my mother to suicide, and was diagnosed with Stage II lung cancer.

It was a long, horrible spiral of terrible events. I turned to schooling to distract me and to bring in extra money. But while in school, a computer glitch resulted in the VA compensation I lived on to be denied to me for two months. I couldn't make rent and was rendered homeless.

My father and I tried homeless shelters, but the effort it took just to get a bed, and to keep people from stealing what little I had, was more than I could bear. I ended up sleeping in my truck at truck stops. At least there were decent people and clean showers there.

But I was at the end of my rope and didn't see a way out. I would find myself staring at my pistol wondering what would happen if I just ended it all. In desperation, my father contacted the local United Way who put me in touch with Volunteers of America, Florida. Volunteers of America convinced me to move back to Oklahoma and directed me to Catholic Charities to sustain me with food, clothing, and suicide counseling until I made it home.

When I arrived in Oklahoma, I spent two days looking for work when I found out about the Mayor's Veteran Council. I showed up in borrowed clothes and stated my desire for work; that same week Volunteers of America in Tulsa contacted me. I assumed it would be for aid but, lo and behold, they offered me a career in something I was passionate about and had ample experience in.

I am still struggling. But thanks to Volunteers of America and their compassionate personnel, I am finally off the street and on my way to financial recovery. ★

CARLOS RODRIQUEZ *is a veteran employment consultant with Volunteers of America Oklahoma.*

"I was at the end of my rope and didn't see a way out."

MEMORIES OF A MINESWEEPER

DONALD A. WEBB

For years I bore a heavy guilt, and I'm glad to share what happened to it.

I was 20 years old, and World War II had just ended. There were still mines in the seas around Britain and France, and I was the navigating officer of a Royal Navy minesweeper. One night, when a thick fog was keeping us in the harbor, we got an S.O.S. from a sinking tanker and we sailed out to help her. My job was to find the tanker so her crew could be brought aboard and the wounded rushed to the hospital. Navigating through dense night fog was difficult, but we found the sinking ship at last.

The wounded were quickly brought below deck, but one sailor was so badly injured they dared not tilt him down a ladder, so they put him in my tiny chart room between my feet. I had to straddle him, one foot on either side. He looked my age.

It was even more difficult finding a way back through that dark fog, now with the pressure of these merchant sailors needing urgent help, especially this enlisted man under my feet. His makeshift bandages were seeping blood, making the deck slippery. The side of his head was caved in. He appeared to have massive internal stomach damage and a broken leg.

He could hardly breathe, but he could still—just—speak. He kept trying to tell me about himself, his home, his Dad, two small sisters, his church. He'd been in the youth choir, or something. I was too busy to answer. Every few minutes, I'd have to put down my instruments and wipe clots of blood from his mouth with my handkerchief. My hands, and the chart, were soon red.

I wished he'd just stop talking. It was punishing, in that fog, finding buoy after buoy. And there was all that blood.

Perhaps it dawned on me, deep down, what he was trying to tell me. He was afraid he was going to die, and he wanted someone to be friendly to him. But if I did suspect it, I never let the thought enter my mind. I may have felt that we wouldn't get everyone ashore in time with him interrupting, bleeding, and whispering.

We were two miles from shore when he died. He asked me for a cigarette, but I was a pipe-smoker. A frightened look came on that bruised face, and his life left him. I navigated the last two miles with my eyes full.

For years, I've been ashamed. He was my brother, and I denied him.

I tell myself I was young then. But so was he. For a long time his scared face would often look up at me and the shame would creep back.

But gradually—mercifully—I found his memory pointing me away from shame and into doing something useful, such as helping veterans suffering from battle trauma or homelessness, or helping disabled folks or disadvantaged youngsters who live in poverty and have no education and no chance unless we help.

So I asked our local Volunteers of America if I could serve with them. And I do, very gratefully. ★

REV. DONALD A. WEBB, PhD, *a Methodist minister, was president of Centenary College of Louisiana, and is a past board member and volunteer with Volunteers of America North Louisiana.*

"Perhaps it dawned on me, deep down, what he was trying to tell me. He was afraid he was going to die, and he wanted someone to be friendly to him."

SELF-INFLICTED MORAL INJURY

EDWARD GRINNAN

It was an unexpected honor to be asked to contribute to this important work on moral injury, yet I had to question my own qualifications to write on the subject. After all, I was not aware of having suffered a moral injury myself or of knowing anyone close to me who might have. But upon researching the condition that indeed afflicts so many, I was stunned to learn that moral injury can be self-inflicted. I had wrongly assumed that a wound to one's conscience could only be caused by another person or a morally traumatic situation. This new understanding led me to examine an experience from my past—from my boyhood, really—that haunts me to this day.

It happened one fall night in early high school, perhaps tenth grade. My family lived in Birmingham, Michigan, an upper-middle class area in the northern suburbs of Detroit. Kids from Birmingham were often derided as privileged snobs and worse, and that reputation was sometimes deserved. My particular subdivision was solidly middle class but there were some truly affluent sections of Birmingham and adjacent Bloomfield

Hills. Mitt Romney, for instance, grew up about a mile from my house seven years ahead of me.

On the night in question, my school, Birmingham Groves, was playing the Redford High football team in Redford. Redford was a more working-class, blue-collar suburb closer to Detroit. But it wasn't far from Birmingham, not geographically at least, and lots of Groves students were headed over to support their Falcons on the gridiron and to have a good time.

A good time. That's what four of my buddies and I were looking for, though our idea of a good time wasn't exactly everybody's. Jim, who had a license and the use of his dad's car, drove us into Detroit to a neighborhood where we could find someone to sell us beer and cigarettes. Then we headed to Redford.

I'm not sure how interested we were in the game itself. We cruised around the stands exchanging good-natured insults with Groves students and smirks with the Redford ones. Then, under the bleachers, we encountered a knot of Redford boys.

They were tough looking, but no tougher than us, I told myself. They laughed at one of my friend's varsity jackets, an invitation to have a conversation, so we kind of faced off. I was by no means the leader of our group but somehow I ended up squared off with the leader of theirs, a guy named Walter in a slick, new, black leather motorcycle jacket. He had made the sarcastic comment about my friend's jacket, and now he was sneering and puffing out his chest, just a few inches from me, this Redford jerk and his jacket.

For a minute or so we taunted each other with remarks about our respective schools. "You're just a bunch of Birmingham brats," said Walter. I lit up a cigarette and immediately felt a little dizzy.

"Oh, yeah?" I said. "Watch this."

"Watch what?"

"I can blow smoke out of my eyes."

"Let's see you."

"Watch my eyes. Watch them."

I took a big drag, and as Walter stared mutely at my eyeballs I surreptitiously maneuvered my cigarette and burned a hole through the left sleeve of his leather jacket. *That should teach him to mouth off.*

I expected there might be some shoving and even a few swings when my dirty trick was discovered. Instead Walter jumped back and gasped. And then he started crying. "My mom is going to kill me! She saved up for this jacket! What am I going to do? She's going to kill me!"

A thunderbolt of guilt struck me. A kind of hysteria welled up within me. I pushed it down. I was not a bully, not at all. I tended to befriend outsiders and outcasts. Walter was the one that I thought acted like a bully. Instead he was wiping tears from his eyes and walking away, sobbing, his downtrodden crew following him into the crisp fall night.

My friends and I laughed and sauntered out to the parking lot to pass around a bottle of Canadian Club, pilfered from Jim's father's liquor cabinet. I got slapped on the back and punched on the shoulder for my fearless display of cunning and toughness. I'd shown those Redford losers!

Inside I cringed. I convulsed. This wasn't me. Just a year earlier I'd been an altar boy. I would have to confess this. It was the only way. It was a horrible, rotten thing to do, and I was a horrible, rotten person for doing it. While my friends whooped and bantered and passed around the bottle, all I could think about were the tears running down Walter's flushed cheeks. Some tough guy he was.

I never did confess it. I was too ashamed. I wanted to hide in my own shadow. And in the course of my life I have made many mistakes and have hurt people I cared about. In other words, I have been perfectly human. I have forgiven myself for my faults and tried to be a better person. Yet for some unfathomable reason, that night in Redford haunted me. I didn't know Walter's last name. I had no way of making it up to him, of explaining to his mother what I had done, how it was all my fault, how I'd be happy to buy him a new jacket. Instead I just ran back to Birmingham, a Birmingham brat.

> "I have made many mistakes and have hurt people I cared about. In other words, I have been perfectly human."

Years later, struggling through my first year of sobriety in AA, I confided the incident to my sponsor. I still felt a bolt of hot shame when I spoke of it. That night was a thorn in my conscience. My well-meaning sponsor chuckled. "It's not like you *stabbed* poor Walter. This is just your disease telling you that you aren't worthy of sobriety. I've done things a million times worse. Trust me, it's just a distraction from your primary purpose."

Maybe. But even now, after many years gratefully free of drugs and alcohol, Walter's face still sometimes appears in my mind's eye. It's like a reminder, a therapist once told me, that all of us can do things contrary to our moral code. We are all capable of doing wrong, even evil. That night in Redford I understood for the first time how my deliberate actions could harm someone else. I didn't want to hurt Walter. I was just showing off. It wasn't so much my action, it was the context. I took advantage of a kid. I broke the rules. I cheated with the cigarette trick. And I reduced this hood to a blubbering mess. I had no right.

Some of you may have the same skeptical reaction as my sponsor—that I am blowing a typical teenage prank, momentarily cruel but basically harmless, into something it's not, into something comparable to an atrocity. But this *was* an atrocity, a very private one, a singular shame. It was as if I lost my innocence about myself that night, as if I had truly sinned for the first time. But I think I finally have a name for what that faceoff under the Redford stands was—a self-inflicted moral injury, a thorn in my conscience that festered for years until I finally realized what to do about it. I brought my secret to God.

As the AA program teaches, I have tried to make direct and sincere amends to the people I have harmed, especially with my drinking and drugging. There are times this is not possible, such as with Walter, whom I never saw again. I have no idea what happened to him. He probably has no particular recollection of that night. Still, I can make amends to him. I must make amends to him, and to the God I hurt, in my heart. Moral injury can be self-inflicted. Even if it is not inflicted on another, even when it is a secret one keeps for years, it is a thorn only a power greater than myself can work free. ★

EDWARD GRINNAN *is editor in chief of Guideposts magazine.*

"Even if it is not inflicted on another, even when it is a secret one keeps for years, it is a thorn only a power greater than myself can work free."

RELEARNING TO LIVE

HANK WARD

My name is Hank Ward, and I am a proud beneficiary of Volunteers of America's guidance and support.

Based on my childhood, I should not have to say that. My mother and father were married and made sure I was well cared for and knew I was loved. I excelled in youth sports and made traveling all-star teams every year. My report cards were full of A's and B's. I attended church on a regular basis. In high school I had good grades, played football, and ran track. I graduated as a member of the National Honor Society, Mu Alpha Theta math honor society, Fellowship of Christian Athletes, and Future Farmers of America. On graduation day, I proudly wore my cap and gown with my honors stole.

I applied for college scholarships but ultimately decided the military was the best choice for me. The National Guard hadn't deployed in many years, and I would be able to go to college almost immediately; at age 17, I was honored to take the oath. I went to basic training in Fort Benning, Georgia, and soon I was crawling through obstacle courses and firing on rifle ranges.

I enrolled in Southern Arkansas University. But I was young, and after tasting the freedom of being out of my parents' house, I quickly became distracted from my studies and dropped out of college. While working and doing my one-weekend-a-month for the National Guard, I received orders—my unit was being activated for deployment to Bosnia. It was a relatively calm deployment but for a single incident that threw the next 10 years of my life into chaos.

I was off-duty in the Rec Center in Bosnia, shooting a game of pool. My buddies and I were laughing and relaxing, and I was lining up my shot on the eight ball for the win. In my sightline, behind that eight ball, was a TV where news of the September 11th attack on the World Trade Center was breaking. I took the shot, but to this day can't remember whether or not I made it in the pocket.

When I finally arrived stateside and returned to civilian life, I got back into the routine of working and weekend duties with the Guard. I even enrolled in college. A few months later, President Bush ordered the invasion of Iraq, and I received new orders.

My unit prepared for worst-case scenarios in Iraq. No one said it aloud, but we all knew what we were about to face was going to be bad. I was the top gunner in our platoon, and I was tasked to be the gunner for the lead vehicle in all of our operations. I felt fear and a nervous churning in my belly as we went outside the perimeter of camp every day during the bloodiest month for American servicemen. Our job was important, so I had to become numb as I lost many friends and saw many Iraqis lose their lives.

We saw things no one should ever see. It is still difficult for me to say.

When I returned home from my tour, I ignored my mental health issues because I just wanted to be with my family. It's a mistake I regret to this day. Life went 90 miles an hour in Iraq, I was on high alert, every minute focused on staying alive. Back home it felt as though everything was going in slow motion.

It was so hard to explain to people how I felt. Symptoms of post-traumatic stress disorder and depression took over. I didn't want to talk to anyone, especially my family and friends. I had nightmares so I stopped sleeping to avoid them. The only time I felt better was when I self-medicated. That was the start of me becoming someone I still don't recognize.

Along with the drug use came the need for money, so I stole things, big things worth thousands of dollars. I sold drugs, bought drugs, stole for drugs, and even stole drugs. I drove my family so far away from me that they told me if I came to their homes they would call the police. At one point, I was arrested for stealing my own truck from the company that repossessed it, and I went to prison. I was out of control and continued to spiral downward. I was ashamed, broke, and homeless. When I

"It was a relatively calm deployment but for a single incident that threw the next 10 years of my life into chaos."

thought about everything I'd done and what I had left to look forward to, I couldn't see any reason to live.

I called my mother one day at four in the morning. I told her I was ready for help and asked her to come get me. On September 11, 2009—eight years after the World Trade Center attacks—my mother drove two hours to pick me up and drove another hour to the VA Medical Center in Shreveport where I was admitted. I needed to relearn how to love myself and live.

After I made it through the detox and substance abuse programs, I was still broke and homeless, but I was determined to change my life.

My treatment team introduced me to the new Volunteers of America, North Louisiana Veteran's Transitional Living Center, and I was one of the first residents admitted to the facility. The partnership between the VA and Volunteers of America was perfect for me. The VA got me back into the habit of working, and Volunteers of America gave me a place to live and got me back into the habit of saving money and paying rent. I was given all the tools I needed to recover and succeed, all I had to do was put them to use. And I did.

Today I tell people the VA got me healthy, and Volunteers of America saved my life.

Since leaving Volunteers of America, I'm very proud to have graduated from Northwest Louisiana Technical College. I took the journeyman electrician test, passed on my first attempt, and now have a job as an electrician at the VA hospital. After the hard work of repairing my credit, I purchased a vehicle. And in 2016, I purchased my own house.

Today I have a job, a little bit of money, my own home, and I have rebuilt relationships with my family. In a little more than six years, I've taken myself from rock bottom to a place where the sky is the limit. I've worked my tail off to get here, but I thank God every day for the generosity of complete strangers that helped me turn my life around. ★

HANK WARD *is an electrician with a VA hospital in Northern Louisiana.*

"I needed to relearn how to love myself and live."

THE DISAPPEARANCE
OF MY WORLD
AS I KNEW IT

JAN BYNUM

Tuesday, July 15, 1997, started out as an ordinary day. I got ready for work, and my daughter, Kelli, was getting ready for her classes at the University of North Texas. I stopped in her room before I left for the office and told her to have a good day.

"I love you," I said. "I'll talk to you this afternoon."

Those were the last words I spoke to my daughter.

Later that day, I received a phone call from Kelli's boyfriend asking if I had heard from her. I told him no. He said Kelli had called him around noon and asked him to come to Denton because the key to her car would not work in the lock and she needed help getting in. When he arrived in Denton, her car was in the parking lot but Kelli was nowhere to be found.

Kelli had been required to tour the Denton City Police Department for her criminal justice class. Ironically, she was parked in the lot across from the police department that day. That was where her car was found with no clue to her whereabouts. It was as if Martians came and lifted her into thin air.

By 5:30 that afternoon, I was certain something was wrong. Kelli was supposed to pick up her daughter, Alexis, from the babysitter's at 5:30. She would never forget to pick up Alexis or not make arrangements for her to be picked up.

My adrenalin was flowing. Every time the phone rang my heart pounded. Then the minutes turned to hours, the hours to days, the days to months, the months to years. It is a parent's worst nightmare to have their child disappear and not know where they are or if they need help. There are no words for the pain.

At some point, I realized I had two choices: dig a hole and crawl in, or pick up and move on. I chose the second option. We were blessed to have Kelli's daughter to raise, which certainly kept me focused. I had a job to do and that job was to raise Alexis. That decision did not take the pain away, but it gave me a reason to go on.

Did I often feel abandoned? Of course I did. And I questioned everything. Kelli was doing her job, raising her daughter, and going to school full-time. She attended class that day, just as instructed. Then she disappeared. I questioned God and wondered how He could let this happen. But I finally got my head and my heart around the reality that God did not do this. Kelli had been in the wrong place at the wrong time and one of God's children used his free will to take Kelli and harm her. God gave me the strength and the tools to get through this ordeal. He put the right people in my life. He taught me to seek help.

On April 11, 2016, I finally learned that my baby was not returning. That was the day they confirmed the identity of her remains, which were uncovered in Brazoria County, Texas. The man responsible for her death led detectives there. She had been abducted, raped and murdered. My hope that she would return was gone. But there was comfort in knowing she was not in harm's way. Kelli was in God's arms and safe, and I am thankful every day that I had twenty years with her.

With this new reality, I faced new challenges. I never had to think about Kelli's disappearance as "final," and now I needed to plan things I never thought about: a funeral, a date of death, cremation, etc. I also wanted to go to Brazoria County to see where my baby had been all these years. Kelli's daughter went with me. The owners of the property and the group of detectives from the police department came to the location to meet us. The property owners and the detectives put a wood fence around the area where Kelli had been buried and they planted flowers. The police department sent a lovely arrangement. They were kind, loving, and caring people, and they served as a reminder that there are many wonderful, good people in this world.

Afterwards, I planned the Celebration of Life Event for Kelli Ann Cox. Kelli was only 20 at the time of her disappearance but she impacted many people. The celebration was at our home in Farmers Branch, Texas, and hundreds of people came by to share memories about Kelli. Many who attended did not know Kelli personally but hearing about her disappearance and her story over the years had an impact on them. At the end of the afternoon, we released balloons in celebration of Kelli's life. It was amazing how the balloons remained grouped together until they were completely out of sight.

In the nearly 20 years since Kelli's disappearance, I've been very open about her story. I share it in hope that it can help someone else. I want people to be aware of their surroundings. I want them to know there is danger in this world. I also want people to know that no matter how unfair something feels it can help if you focus on the good. I want something good to come out of our horrible tragedy.

I beat myself up over the years because I questioned God and His actions, but I know my feelings were, and are, normal. God put the right people in my path and it was up to me to let them in, which I did. That was hard for me to do because I would think *what can someone else do? Can they find Kelli?* Maybe not, but letting others in not only helped me, it helped others know they could survive tragedies in life. I told many people, "Just because there is a tragedy in your life, the world does not stop. Life goes on." Some people may believe that sounds harsh, but it is reality. And with faith and support you can—and will—survive a tragedy or trauma.

Kelli was born November 12, 1976 at Baylor Hospital in Dallas, Texas. She was one month late and weighed in at a whopping 10 pounds. She is my only child.

She was an excellent student through elementary school and middle school— a very good student in high school. She was very active in gymnastics and was a cheerleader in the 7th and 8th grades. When we first found out Kelli was pregnant, I told her I wanted her to finish school. I agreed to pay for her school as long as she kept up her grades. I explained that she could not go off to school because what we would have spent on room and board would be spent helping to raise her baby. I remember Kelli looking at me and saying, "Mom, that is more than fair."

She certainly kept up her end of the bargain. Alexis was born on a Monday, and one week later Kelli was back at college taking her final exams for the semester. She made straight A's. She was enrolled in another six hours at the time of her disappearance.

> "I realized I had two choices: dig a hole and crawl in, or pick up and move on. I chose the second option."

Kelli was very determined to stay on schedule and finish school in a timely fashion, but that was the deal we made. And while she was carrying a full load in college, she was also responsible with Alexis: tending to all of Alexis' needs, taking her to doctor's appointments, shopping for her, bathing her, running errands with her, doing her laundry, sharing in the general household duties. Kelli had the patience of Job and remarkable maturity. She also had a great sense of humor. She was funny, sensitive, smart, athletic, and headstrong. We all miss her terribly. Kelli was not only lovely on the outside, but also lovely on the inside.

The greatest crime of all is that Alexis did not get to know her mom and that Kelli did not get to know her daughter. We have tried our best, but there is no replacement for that bond between a mother and daughter.

I know only too well. ★

JAN BYNUM *is a retired Volunteers of America Texas minister.*

"God put the right people in my path and it was up to me to let them in, which I did."

MORAL INJURY

A Brief Perspective About the Holocaust

JENNI FRUMER

My father escaped the Holocaust. At just 18-months-old he arrived in South Africa from Panevėžys, Lithuania, with his mother and four siblings. My grandfather joined them a few months later in 1939. During the Nazi occupation, nearly the entire Jewish population of Panevėžys was murdered in 1943; only a few managed to escape and find asylum abroad. The local Lithuanian police assisted in the executions of least 7,523 Jews by Nazi Germans.

My earliest memories growing up in South Africa are of being surrounded by thick Yiddish accents, but it was not until I attended Jewish day school and was exposed to graphic pictures of the slave labor, death camps, and ghettos, that I began to fully understand the morality—or lack thereof—of "man's inhumanity to man." By age 16, I knew I would commit myself to working within the Jewish community; by 19 I was determined to work with older adults, Holocaust survivors in particular, to ensure the age with dignity.

In retrospect, it has been my own life-long desire to understand my own deep reactions to the Holocaust, which could be identified as shame and guilt. I continue to have conflicted thoughts and, for years, have attempted to comprehend the despair

I experience from "vicarious trauma" or "secondary trauma" (Bride, 2007 and Kellerman, 2001) as a result of my family's narratives and from my professional work with Holocaust survivors over the past 35 years.

THE HOLOCAUST

The Holocaust refers to a dark period in history during the Second World War. Also known as the Shoah (the Hebrew word for "catastrophe") or by the Greek words hólos ("whole") and kaustós ("burnt"). Under the Nazi regime, the Jews, and other targeted populations and groups, were murdered. Hitler considered the Jews, in particular, "vermin," which culminated in the "Final Solution"—the mass genocide and extermination all Jews in Europe. More than six million Jews were murdered during the Holocaust, including 1.5 million children.

The international definition of a Holocaust survivor is any Jew who was displaced during the years of 1933–1945. While professionals often generalize about the collective experience of Holocaust survivors, we must not forget their individual stories. Nor should we overlook the effects of moral injury as a result of their proximity to death and/or witnessing or causing trauma, which may have been necessary to function within highly complex and unpredictable situations.

Not all Holocaust survivors lived through the horrors of concentration and death camps. During the Holocaust, thousands of Jewish adults and children survived against all odds in countless ways, including: assuming different identities, fighting against the Nazi regime and its Allies as Partisans, hiding in forests and caves, being hidden by locals at great risk of the locals and escaping by hiking the Pyrenes Mountains in winter. Some were forced to perform acts of cruelty or to act in shameful ways in order to survive.

Regardless of each survivor's unique Holocaust experience, all Jews displaced during those years were victims of Nazi trauma. The forced deportation of millions and the atrocities of Hitler's Final Solution were—and remain—beyond comprehension. But for more than 50 years following the War, there was a *Conspiracy of Silence* during which the diaspora (the world) refused to acknowledge those atrocities.

> "While professionals often generalize about the collective experience of Holocaust survivors, we must not forget their individual stories."

TRIGGERS AND TRAUMA

The median age of living Holocaust survivors is 87. Survivors experience aging as other adults do, with declining physical functioning and other health issues. But they can also experience fear and distress triggered by Holocaust memories as they deal with aging-related issues. Triggers may be physical, emotional, environmental, or situational, such as: bright lights, being told go "to the shower," barking dogs, natural hunger pangs, medical procedures, holidays, feeling cold, or being asked to fill out a medical history form in a physician's office. These are only some of the everyday occurrences that may activate visceral reactions in Holocaust survivors related to past trauma.

It is critical for professionals to be culturally competent in the support and care of Holocaust survivors and their families. When assisting patients, healthcare professionals must contain their own feelings and refrain from making moral and social judgements when they hear about a survivor's experience, as their behavior may run counter to their own norms and expectations of society. As a professional, I recognize how privileged I am to serve Holocaust survivors. I have learned how passivity and feelings of disempowerment may contribute to feelings of moral injury or increasing despair over time (Shay, 2014).

STORIES OF MORAL INJURY*

Mr. Davidovich is a 90-year-old Holocaust survivor who receives support from the Holocaust Survivor Assistance program at Alpert Jewish Family & Children's Services (AJFCS). He resides alone in West Palm Beach. During the Holocaust he survived many labor and concentration camps. He describes himself at the beginning of the war as a strong 16-year-old. He points to his hands and says, "You see these hands . . . they saved me." He recalls a normal childhood and constantly states: "Nothing prepared us for what we saw." He has experienced lifelong nightmares. He repeats his stories and describes in detail an incident that occurred when he was assigned to a labor battalion to dig a ditch. He explains that it was cold and pouring rain and full of mud. He describes how another young man slipped and fell into the hole the group was digging and how he begged the others to help him pull the helpless young man out. In all the commotion, a Nazi guard walked over, shot the young man in the ditch, and ordered the others in the group to bury him. Mr. Davidovich continues to experience guilt, shame, and anger—the moral injury—from this and other experiences during the Holocaust.

* *Names and demographics have been changed to maintain client confidentiality.*

Mrs. Goldstone is an 84-year-old widowed Holocaust survivor. She was 19 when the war started, and she survived several concentration camps with her mother. She recalls the shock of arriving at the first camp and the noise and commotion. She talks about the wailing of young mothers separated from their babies and how she's continued to hear their cries throughout her entire life. When she became a mother herself, she would wake after regular nightmares then run into her children's bedrooms to ensure they were still safe. She continues to have separation concerns in regard to her children, grandchildren and great grandchildren, even though she and her mother were liberated from Bergen-Belsen. She still acutely grieves the death of her mother who died a few days after liberation after being "overfed" by their well-meaning liberators; the circumstances of her mother's death resulted in Mrs. Goldstone's life-long inability to trust. She demonstrates the effects of moral injury in that she has "never been able to turn off" what she witnessed. She experiences daily feelings of shame, anxiety, and guilt for not doing more to save those children who were separated from their mothers at the train platform. She is unable to reconcile her intense anger for trusting liberating soldiers who, in spite of their good intentions, "killed" her mother.

> "She demonstrates the effects of moral injury in that she has 'never been able to turn off' what she witnessed."

A greater understanding of the effects of moral injury helps inform us of the impact of the experiences of trauma survivors. It also reinforces for me, how a "trustworthy clinical community and, particularly, a well-functioning clinical team [can] provide protection for clinicians and are a major factor in successful outcomes with morally injured" Holocaust survivors (Shay, 2014, p. 182). ★

JENNI FRUMER, PHD *is the Chief Executive Officer at the Ferd & Gladys Alpert Jewish Family & Children's Service in West Palm Beach, FL., and wishes to thank Sara Zenlea, LCSW, AJFCS Holocaust survivor care coordinator, for her contribution to this essay.*

REFERENCES

Baycrest Health Sciences Practice Manual.
*Caring for Aging Holocaust Survivors:
A Practice Manual.* Retrieved: http://
www.baycrest.org/about/publications/
caregivers/caring-for-aging-survivors-of-
the-holocaust/

Bride, B. (2007). Prevalence of secondary
traumatic stress among social workers.
Social Work, 52, 1, 63-70.

Holocaust Atlas of Lithuania. Retrieved:
http://www.holocaustatlas.lt/EN/#a_atlas/
search/vcntfr=5000/page/1/item

Kellerman, N. (2001). Psychopathology
in children of Holocaust survivors:
A review of the research literature. *The
Israel Journal of Psychiatry and Related
Sciences, 38, 1,* 36-46.

Shay, J. (2014). Moral Injury. *Psychoanalytic
Psychology, 31, 2,* 182-191.

Tedeschi, R. & Calhoun, L. (2006) *Handbook
of Posttraumatic Growth: Research and
Practice.* Mahwah, NJ: Lawrence Erlbaum
Associates, 11-13.

ALL THE CHILDREN OF THE WORLD

JIM WALLIS

My personal experience with moral injury happened as I entered adolescence in the 1960s in Detroit. I have never called it "moral injury," but I think it applies.

This Detroit was two communities: one white and one black, separate and dramatically unequal. Growing up white in Detroit, I had no exposure to black people but for an occasional glimpse on a downtown bus or at a Tigers baseball game. What I was told about African Americans was based on stereotypes common in white culture back then.

As a teenager, I felt the tension and hostility that pervaded the conversations among whites whenever the subject of blacks, race, the city, or crime came up. People I knew to otherwise be kind and loving would be transformed, uttering vicious words of intolerance and fearful hatred.

I wanted to know why. Why did whites and blacks live completely divided from one another? Why was I hearing so much about the differences between white and black Detroit when it came to wealth, work, schools, police, and so many other things. What created the hostility and fear? I was persistent in taking my questions to my parents, teachers, and friends, but I soon discovered that no one could provide me with answers. "You're too young to ask these questions," they said. "You will understand when you get older. We don't know why it's this way, but it always has been."

Hoping that the church might provide some answers, I asked: "What about our Christian faith? Doesn't God love all people? When I look around me, why do I only see white children?" I reminded the people in my church of a song I was taught in Sunday school as a child: *Jesus loves the little children, all the children of the world; red and yellow, black and white, all are precious in his sight; Jesus loves the little children of the world.*

Of course, the song is true and God loves everybody, I was told, but there are differences. And, of course, we love everybody too but that doesn't mean we have to live together.

I asked the church people why we sent missionaries to Africa but didn't have any contact with black people in our own city. Weren't there a lot of black Christians and churches too? Why didn't our churches ever have anything to do with one another?

I was told that we were better off separated. Some even used the Bible to undergird their argument, citing the Genesis story in which Noah curses the descendants of his son Ham. Others said that blacks were happy with the way things were. They had their ways and places to live, and we had ours. There should be no problems. And if they had problems, they probably deserved them.

Some people told me that asking these questions would only get me into trouble. That proved to be the only honest answer I ever got.

It didn't take long to realize that I wasn't going to get the answers I was looking for from white people, so I decided to make my way from the suburbs to the city.

My church was a small evangelical one called Plymouth Brethren. The first thing I discovered, to my great surprise, was that there were black Plymouth Brethren assemblies in inner-city Detroit. They were just like my church in most ways, right down to the same dreadful hymnbook, and I wondered why I had never been told about them. I visited the churches and sought out the elders and learned that they had known about our assemblies for years. Most even recognized my name because of the role my father played in the white assemblies; some had even met him.

As I asked my questions, a new world opened up. Here were black church leaders making time in their very busy lives for a young white kid, full of questions, who had come to see them in the city. They were extraordinarily patient and receptive, never patronizing and always compassionate. They must have been smiling inside at my idealism and the questions, which had obvious answers, but they never let on.

I believed if black and white Christians would simply pray and examine the Bible together, they would learn to love one another and begin to see change. I was excited at the prospect. We planned on scheduling meetings with people in the white churches. I learned later that the black leaders had been through all this before.

I'm sure I was so aggressive in setting up the meetings that the white Christians didn't know what to do except go along with the scheme. I will never forget our first get-together—in a white church, of course, because my white friends weren't about to go into the inner city. I can still see the polite, frozen smiles on their faces as they awkwardly shook hands with my new black friends.

There were not many meetings, and the idea soon died out. The interest was always genuine from the black Christians, though I'm not sure why they were still willing to try after all the abuse they had endured from white Christians. Our guests were open and reconciling in their posture; there were no angry words or militant spirits from these gracious saints.

My favorite was Bill Pannell, then a young leader in the black Plymouth Brethren assemblies who ultimately became a professor and Dean of the Chapel at Fuller Theological Seminary. I was deeply touched by reading Bill's book *My Friend, the Enemy*, a painful and articulate account of his experience growing up black in white America. I felt especially hurt by his recounting of the racism of white churches.

Bill's was not the only book I read. I devoured everything I could get my hands on written by or about black people and racism in America. I was inspired by Rev. Dr. Martin Luther King Jr.'s speeches and books. *The Autobiography of Malcolm X* became one of the most influential books of my life. The simple, self-justifying worldview of my childhood and my church, conflicting with my growing awareness of racism and poverty, caused mounting havoc in my teenage years. I was shocked at what I read and felt betrayed and angry at the brutal facts of racism. Worse, I felt implicated.

I began to seek more opportunities for interaction and dialogue, especially with young black workers and students. Over several summers, I took jobs as a machine operator in a small factory, then on custodial and maintenance crews in Detroit office buildings. The blacks I met were much more angry and bitter than the black Christians I had come to know. They provided me with a new education.

Butch was typical of the young, bright members of Detroit's urban poor. Butch and I worked together as janitors at Detroit Edison the summer before I went off to college. Our lives were as different as the destinations of our paychecks. I was

"I was shocked at what I read and felt betrayed and angry at the brutal facts of racism. Worse, I felt implicated."

still living at home, so my salary went into a savings account for college. His went to support his wife, mother, sisters and brothers, who all lived together in a small place in one of Detroit's worst neighborhoods. His father had passed away, so a lot fell on Butch.

According to the executives and their secretaries at Detroit Edison, the difference in the color of our skin meant Butch and I merited different treatment. Their race and class bias was blatant. I was often put on moving crews with Butch and the other blacks who worked there. At best, they were regarded as men with strong backs and no heads; at worst, as beasts of burden. Nineteen-year-old white office secretaries ordered them around, complaining constantly about their work.

The resentment among the custodial crew went very deep. After a while, some of them trusted me enough to talk openly in my presence about the hatred they felt for the system and those who ran it.

Butch and I were often put on elevator duty together. We had to endure an insufferable barrage of bad jokes from the upper-echelon workers such as, "Bet this job has its ups and downs," and, "You're moving up faster than anyone in this whole company." We were instructed to be polite and humor the people. But I never had to suffer the patronizing tone that always greeted Butch. I received instant respect because it was known that I was soon to be a university student and had every opportunity to one day be one of them.

Butch was very savvy about the streets, the job, Detroit, and politics. His education came from the pages of the perpetual string of books he kept tucked in the back pocket of his khaki janitor's uniform. His experience of oppression, and his reflections on it, were turning him into a political revolutionary. He was very committed to the worldwide black liberation struggle, and he knew as much about African history as I did about American. My growing political awareness was bringing my convictions in line with his.

The job gave us the opportunity to spend hours together. We had many of our best conversations in the elevators. Elevator operators are required by law to get periodic breaks, as going up and down all day without a respite begins to make one's head spin. But mine was already reeling with all the thoughts and ideas Butch was helping nurture along, so I spent all my breaks in his elevator and he spent his in mine.

Butch and I talked about everything: our backgrounds, our families and neighborhoods, our churches. We discussed black consciousness, the police, and the suburbs. We lived in the same city, but I was learning that we grew up in two different countries.

Eventually, Butch invited me to come to his home and meet his family. I felt deeply honored and very eager to go. But every time I asked him to write directions to his place, he would change the subject. Finally one day with pen and paper in hand, I sat him down and said, "Look, Butch, how do you expect me to get to your house if you don't write out directions for me?"

Awkwardly, he began to scribble on the paper. When I realized the reason he hesitated before was because he could barely write, I was ashamed at my insensitivity.

That small incident was very significant to me. I went home that night and cried and cursed. I could not believe someone as bright as Butch had not been taught to write. I was furious at a system that had given me so much and him almost nothing simply by virtue of our skin color. By accident of birth, I had all the benefits and he all the suffering. I vowed to do everything I could to change that system.

On the appointed evening, I went to Butch's house. All but Butch's youngest brothers and sisters were nervous and suspicious of a white man in their home. Almost from the moment I sat down, the youngest ones were in my lap, smiling, their bright eyes sparkling at a newfound friend. But the older they were, the deeper the hurt and distrust in their eyes. I stayed for several hours. When the older ones realized I really was a friend to Butch, they began to open up.

I was especially taken by Butch's mother. She was a lovely woman, gracious and warm, so anxious for me to feel at home. She was just like my mother in so many ways. She wasn't interested in politics, was certainly not militant, and would never have been mistaken for a radical. She was concerned about the same things my mother was: the health, happiness, and safety of her family—and the growth of her son's radical ideas.

I asked Butch's mother about her past, her experiences in Detroit, her family. She had a way of looking into your eyes and speaking right to your heart. I knew I was hearing the honest reflections of a proud woman who had somehow kept her family together through the difficulties of growing up black in Detroit. She recounted a history of poverty and abuse. She told of countless times her husband or one of her sons had been picked up on the street

"I was furious at a system that had given me so much and him almost nothing simply by virtue of our skin color."

by the police for no apparent reason, taken down to the precinct, falsely accused, verbally abused, and even beaten.

She would go down every time to find out what had happened and try to bring them home. Each time she was assaulted with vile and profane language. The police would tell her they would "take care of her husband or son and give her man what he deserved," and that she'd "better get her ass on home or she was going to get the same treatment."

My insides began to hurt and I became tearful as every person in the room told me stories of how they or their close friends had been abused by the police for being at the wrong place at the wrong time and for being black. I realized that the reputation that the Detroit police had for brutalizing black people had been earned.

Something Butch's mother said that night stayed with me for the rest of my life. She told her kids, "If you are ever lost and see a policeman, duck under a stairwell or hide behind a building and wait until he passes. Then come out and find your way home by yourself." My mother's words to her five kids echoed in my head, "If you are ever lost and can't find you way home, look for a policeman. The policeman is your friend and he will take you by the hand and bring you home safely." My mother told us to seek out policemen; Butch's mother told her children to avoid them.

Butch's mom and family helped show me the other America, the America that is unfair and wrong and mean and hateful, the America that white people accepted. But they taught me about more than racism. They taught me about love and family and courage, about what is most important and what it means to be a human being. In listening to the black experience, I discovered more truth about myself, my country, and my faith than by listening anywhere else.

I felt a deep sense of betrayal by white America. I was disillusioned with my country and my upbringing as never before. My burning question became: Why hadn't I been told?

White America kept itself isolated and protected and successfully hid the truth until the late 1960s when the riots began.

For a long time I tried to get my church to deal with the issue of racism. After the riots, the people of the church finally agreed to take up the subject. Even then it was relegated to a midweek, night meeting rather than a Sunday morning.

"They taught me about love and family and courage, about what is most important and what it means to be a human being."

The format of the meeting was a panel discussion, and I was to take "the side of the blacks." Two of the church's elders were selected to take the other side, the "white point of view." The fourth panelist was a young social worker who was new to the church and sympathetic to the black perspective.

I never prepared harder for anything in my life. My presentation was chock-full of unemployment figures, housing statistics, facts about poverty, welfare, inadequate education and health care, and police brutality. It was also overflowing with Bible verses that dealt with God's love for the poor, concern for justice, and the reconciling work of Christ.

I shared what I learned from blacks about their experience of being poor, segregated, and disenfranchised. The social worker buttressed my argument with more facts and stories from his experience in social work.

The response from the two elders was predictable. One spoke of how his Scottish grandparents had pulled themselves up from their bootstraps as immigrants to America, and he asked why blacks couldn't do the same. The other spent his time defending the American way of life, praising the virtues of capitalism. They failed to engage with anything I had said.

The discussion was then opened up to the congregation, and I hoped the conversation would improve. The first question set the tone for the evening. One of the adults who had known me since birth directed his question to me: "But, Jamie, would you really want your sister, Barbie, to marry one?"

It got worse from there. Most people refused to look at the suffering of black people. One after another, members of the congregation rose to defend themselves, their church, and white America.

By the end of the evening I was thoroughly discouraged and likely, "injured." Only my parents and the wife of the young social worker expressed any real support. People who had known me all my life approached me afterward to offer a string of empty, patronizing remarks about how impressed they were with my presentation and how smart I had become—yet none of them responded to anything I had said.

I painfully remember what one of the church elders said to me that night: "Son, you've got to understand, Christianity has nothing to do with racism. Racism is political, our faith is personal."

That conversation had a dramatic effect on me. It was a real conversion experience, but one that took me out of the church. If the things that were consuming my head and heart had nothing to do with Christianity, then I wanted nothing to do with Christianity. It was a privatized faith that I was raised with, and I wanted it no more. As the church people sought to justify themselves and the country they loved, that country and church seemed uglier and uglier to me.

My alienation from the church over the issue of racism developed into anger by the time I went off to Michigan State University. I had little to do with the church after I left home, but on the occasional weekend when I returned, I paid a visit on Sunday morning to appease my parents.

I had become an angry young man, especially about the hypocrisy of the church, and I continued to drift further and further away from Christian faith. My alienation from the church became complete by the Vietnam War, which I opposed and became a leader in the student movements of my time.

It was years before I was drawn back to Jesus, and I came to see that it was the gospel that spoke to the questions that burned in my heart with more power and authority than anything else. I discovered that the very people my church had kept at arm's length were the ones in whom Jesus was so present. "Whatever you did for one of the least of these brothers and sisters of mine, you did for me," says Matthew 25:40, which became my conversion text.

As a teenager, I didn't have the words to explain what happened to me that night with my church elder, but I found them later: God is always personal, but never private. Trying to understand the public meaning of personal faith has been my vocation ever since. ★

JIM WALLIS *is founder and president of Sojourners, a nonprofit organization whose mission is to inspire hope and build a movement to transform individuals, communities, the church, and the world.*

> "God is always personal, but never private."

SURVIVING WAR & WONDERING WHAT IF?

JIM ZENNER

Forward Operating Base Echo in Al Diwaniyah, Iraq was much quieter than it had been when we arrived a month earlier.

The base was part of a multinational coalition force led by a Polish Commander, but there were soldiers from around the world, including Mongolia, El Salvador, Georgia, and Poland.

I remember stories about the Mongolian troops and how they were no longer allowed to go on patrols because they would spray rounds in every direction every time there was contact. It was also rumored that they would attempt to shoot incoming mortar rounds out of the sky with the AK47s. We all had respect for their eagerness and motivation.

Our taskforce was ordered to invade Al Diwaniyah, to quell the indirect attacks on FOB Echo, and to take back the Area of Operations. The local insurgents learned quickly that RPGs, grenades, RPKs, and AK47s were no match for an aggressive Stryker Cavalry Squadron. In less than a week, our unit had quelled the indirect attacks and began gathering intelligence to start grabbing high-value individuals. We were very effective.

I was raised Catholic from Sunday school to First Communion. I went through Confirmation with Our Lady of Good Counsel in a small town near Mt. Rainier, Washington. I grew up in a log cabin in Mt. Rainier National Park with a wood stove as the only heat source.

I was a shy kid and never much for hanging out with a lot of people. It was probably because I grew up in the woods and spent most of my time playing alone. Once, when

I was little, I threw a pine cone at a squirrel and hit it. I felt so badly I rushed to tell a Park Ranger.

My family was very close. My dad spent a lot of time teaching me and playing baseball with me. Everyone in my family made a big deal out of my baseball seasons, and we'd load up in the station wagon as soon as my dad got home and take off together. We always ate and prayed together.

After our mission was complete in Al Diwaniyah, we were getting ready to section patrol the FOB. The convoy behind us got hit on Main Supply Route Tampa on the way down, so I decided to take off my kit, jump down off our vehicle, and call my wife before we left.

As I was talking to my wife, the Laundromat about 10 to 15 meters behind the call center took a direct hit from a 107mm rocket. It took a second to get out of the small building and run to up to the laundry building that was now in flames.

A Polish soldier and I began throwing water on the fire and we could hear a lady moaning in the building. I tried to get to her but the flames were all the way out to the T-walls—it was like walking into a firebrick oven.

The fire team was on scene, and I was ordered to stop throwing water on the fire by a higher-ranking officer. I told him the team was on the wrong end of the building because someone was dying on this end. He repeated his order more loudly, so I went back to my truck, hopped in the turret, and watched as the lady burned to death. I took pictures. I'm not sure why, but I did.

While I was watching the building burn, I wondered about the woman's parents and how they would take the news. I wondered where she was from. I felt nothing. I still don't remember anything from our convoy all the way back to Baghdad.

For several years I carried a case of the "What Ifs" with me—a phenomenon that many of us veterans dealing with moral injury play over in our heads. It's not a "fear response," but a shattering of the image of self or value. "I am a protector" doesn't necessarily compute anymore once people around you die. My own example is the several years I questioned myself for not going in to drag the woman out before being given my order. In more extreme cases, taking the life of non-enemy combatants in the heat of the moment can impact a person's view of themselves greatly.

Through my work as a social worker with post 9/11-veterans, I have had many veterans write "impact statements," which discuss how their experiences in combat affect how they see themselves, others, and the world. Many veterans describe themselves in a very dark light because of decisions they made, orders they followed, and, in some cases, actions they were neither ordered nor forced to take. One veteran described himself as a monster. It's heartbreaking.

Many soldiers must follow orders that ultimately lead to the death of others. In some cases the soldier doesn't know the person killed, other times that person is the soldier's best friend or someone the soldier is close to. The intent behind the order varies. Nevertheless, the act itself often leaves veterans mistrustful of others, angry with themselves for not making a different decision, and angry with the individual who gave the order.

This is a part of surviving war. Perhaps our lack of understanding of moral injury is why so many of our service members and veterans commit suicide. I know the concept of moral injury has resonated with many veterans I have run into, and I think it is definitely deserving of additional research. ★

JIM ZENNER *is associate director of community programs for the Steven A. Cohen Military Family Clinic at the University of Southern California.*

"'I am a protector' doesn't necessarily compute anymore once people around you die."

GROUNDHOG DAY

KIM CAMPBELL

Living with someone suffering from mild cognitive impairment (MCI) or Alzheimer's disease can make you feel like you are in the movie "Groundhog Day." In the unforgettable 1993 comedy starring Bill Murray and Andie MacDowell, Murray plays Phil Connors, a TV weatherman who finds himself caught in an endlessly repeating time loop, reliving the same day of his life over and over again. From the moment his radio-alarm goes off in the morning, Murray's character knows every detail of the day ahead because he has already lived it hundreds of times before.

Many people caring for someone with Alzheimer's disease say that they strongly identify with the film because they feel like they are living the same day again and again, answering the same questions over and over, holding the same conversations again and again, going through the same routines endlessly, always coming to the same frustrating conclusions—only to wake up the next morning and start all over again. Like Connors predicts: "It's gonna be cold, it's gonna be gray, and it's gonna last you for the rest of your life."

Since Murray's character has no choice but to live the same day over endlessly, he begins to experiment with different strategies to end his unhappiness. For a while he indulges in hedonism, then he tries to better himself by learning piano or mastering sculpture and other educational pursuits, and even attempts suicide more than once.

Eventually, he reexamines his priorities and discovers joy, purpose, and meaning by simply using each new day as an opportunity to help others.

Instead of seeing my life as a caregiver as repetitive drudgery, I began to see each day as another chance to honor my husband in the most meaningful way possible, by fulfilling my vow to love him "in sickness and in health." I pushed aside my own pain, hugged Glen, and told him that I loved him every day regardless of whether or not he understood who I was or what I was saying.

I began connecting with other caregivers across the country by phone and by joining a local support group, and I got involved in advocacy to raise funds for a cure. Like Murray, I also started making time to improve myself by reading books, listening to lectures, taking dance classes, and trying to learn to cook. (I failed at the last of these but am hoping to tackle it again soon.)

The trick to surviving life as an Alzheimer's caregiver is to learn to appreciate each day and use it to help others. Doing this will help you find meaning, joy, and peace in your own life.

Bill Murray's character would not have discovered this truth if he had not found himself caught in an endlessly repeating cycle of reliving the same day over and over again. Likewise, if a caregiver is caught in the time loop long enough, the things that really matter in life become clear. It's not easy, and I wouldn't wish it on anyone, but in some ways, Alzheimer's can be a gift. Watching memory and life slip away from a loved one teaches important lessons in gratitude, compassion and empathy.

> "Instead of seeing my life as a caregiver as repetitive drudgery, I began to see each day as another chance to honor my husband in the most meaningful way possible."

"Groundhog Day" helped me change my perspective on the frustrating repetitiveness that often accompanies Alzheimer's, and I strongly suggest that all caregivers give it a watch if they haven't already. ★

KIM CAMPBELL *was married to country/pop star Glen Campbell for 35 years until his passing in August 2017 following a long and very public battle with Alzheimer's disease. Kim continues to honor Glen's legacy and mission to educate the world about Alzheimer's and its effect on the entire family through the CareLiving Foundation, which she founded to improve the quality of life for caregivers through education, advocacy, and real-world change.*

This article was originally posted on the www.CareLiving.org website on October 1, 2017.

"The trick to surviving life as an Alzheimer's caregiver is to learn to appreciate each day and use it to help others."

ARE CAREGIVERS VICTIMS OF MORAL INJURY?

MERYL COMER

Alzheimer's disease currently affects a reported 5.4 million people in the United States and 44 million worldwide. But there are also 15 million caregivers, just like me, who are unintended victims and not among the official count.

Add to our legions those caring for loved ones with stroke, diabetes, post-traumatic stress, or depression and complicated by a memory disorder. We speak the same language on the front lines of care. The intensity of providing care over years and our 24/7 hyper-vigilance puts our own health and emotional wellbeing in harm's way. Does that qualify as moral injury? Hear me out because I never considered this issue when writing my book, "*Slow Dancing With A Stranger: Lost and Found in the Age of Alzheimer's*" (excerpted in italics).

> *I am his wife, co-pilot and guardian. This once intelligent man has lost his navigational compass. All social filters have been stripped away; the improprieties embarrassing, frightening and explosive. Like clues to the Da Vinci Code, I search and pick up hints he drops while fearing my own safety. A nervous body tick means he needs the bathroom. His eyes are closed, but I take no chances; a clenched fist is an alert I need to find a safe zone. I am in pain for and with him; a suspended state of self-preservation, a discipline hard-learned over years by living intimately in the disease. Hope in the hopelessness of his disease forces me to modulate my metrics for success. I declare small victories at the end of every day so I can meet the next crisis to blindside me with resolve.*

Please tell me: Am I in denial about moral injury? Are the wounds I bear self-inflicted—the result of both choice and forgetting that I matter too?

First and foremost, it is my instinctive and chosen mission to protect his dignity. His illness is not contagious, but our universe of friends has evaporated as if the plague has visited our door. The person they knew is lost, but not gone. Our isolation is our intimacy. I live in the disease with him, fill in the blanks, calm his adrenalin-fueled rage, and pretend that his fate and our life together are not doomed. Unfortunately, I know better.

No one should be surprised by this conundrum. Caregivers are invisible to the medical and faith-based communities, even though our own health is being compromised in our service to others. Have our faith leaders not been adequately trained or do they lack the time to minister to individuals and their families around such an open-ended and unrelenting disease like Alzheimer's?

There is also the unwelcome paternalism of the medical profession. Fifty-five percent of those living with the disease go undiagnosed. Many clinicians miss the symptoms, too often dismiss a family's concern, or consciously prefer not to diagnose to avoid depressing their patients.

Doctors were the ones who kept telling me privately that my husband couldn't last long. Their words strengthened my resolve to see him through to the end. More than two decades later, closure still seems far away.

More than 75 percent of families try to keep a loved one at home. Is that an expression of traditional values or the economics of necessity? Either way, no one can be prepared for the enigma of dementing diseases that challenge families in unimaginable ways.

I am now in my 22nd year caring for both my husband and mother at home. I used to think of myself as the well spouse, but now I realize this isn't the case. My vulnerabilities are great. When people hear my story, they sometimes tell me they wouldn't make the same choices. I do not hold myself up as an example to follow. No one who has been on the front lines of care ever questions when someone says, "I can't do it anymore." On the other hand, "No one deserves to be forgotten in life because their disease is without hope."

"Caregivers are invisible to the medical and faith-based communities, even though our own health is being compromised in our service to others."

Interlocking systems of indifference in America, compounded by stigma and the politics of ageism, represent the current state of affairs for those living with Alzheimer's and their caregivers. We know this all too well as the healthcare debate rages on and prompts fundamental questions around the issue of "do no harm." But how well do the social norms and our health care system accommodate change of status—from well and productive, to mild cognitive impairment, and through later-stage disease progression that may take from three to 20 years? Does society's reaction to getting old with Alzheimer's count as moral injury? It is in the detail of our lives, and the very personal online exchanges, that lay bare the moral dilemma.

From an e-mail exchange with a friend:

"I was surprised at dinner when you asked me, 'Do you take care of your husband out of love or a sense of responsibility?' Let me just say that I love my husband, but I have cared for him all these years with the unconditional love one gives a sick child. Alzheimer's is confounding and cruel. Savor whatever is left of life together with your lovely wife. Please feel free to ask me anything."

His reply: "Excuse my blunt question. It is a question I struggle with myself, which is why I ask. The woman I live with is becoming less and less the woman I fell in love with and married. How must my relationship evolve? I asked you because you have had almost three times longer to think about it. I also asked you because I believe you will tell me what is real, not what is 'correct.' Your parallel with a child resonates with me. I have felt I have a child, whom I can never neglect, that gets younger every year and so needs more and more help, a child in reverse."

Is it the stigma of this disease that marginalizes and sequesters us behind closed doors? New research shows that empathy shuts down if you believe someone is responsible for their own suffering. We must be careful not to insult our parents' generation by inferring that lifestyle changes might have saved them. We did not choose Alzheimer's. The disease attacked my husband's brain and our entire family became its victim too.

Studies have shown that caring for a person with dementia causes more severe health effects, physical and psychological, than other types of caregiving. The greatest fear for many caregivers is that if we break down from physical or mental stress, there is no Plan B. There is no buffer between an infirmed or burnt out AD caregiver and institutional care for a loved one.

A fellow advocate, caring for a wife with early-onset Alzheimer's, writes: "I confess that I was not familiar with the term 'moral injury.' There is certainly an overlap of symptoms. I ask myself whether moral injury resulted from my ten years of caregiving or by my recent decision to put my own life first despite the courage of my wife as she struggles with her disease, the kindness to others that she still can demonstrate, or the smile on her face when I come home. I am still a huge presence in what is left of her life even as she becomes a less and less significant part of mine. Will my efforts to reinvigorate my own life leave me scarred by moral injury? My own kids said they could see how quickly I was deteriorating because of stress and lack of sleep. They respected my choice to care for my wife but argued that I was sacrificing my life. Will it be better or worse for her daughter who has made it clear that she will institutionalize her mother if something happens to me? There is a clear moral dilemma for caregivers. Aren't we morally injured no matter which choice we make?"

Although we often focus on moral injury as something that occurs in military combat, it is said to be a much broader phenomenon that may follow any severe trauma as it undermines not only the individual, but familial and intergenerational bonds.

Am I blind to "moral injury" because I see no way out unless I declare defeat? Every day I ask myself if I am doing anything that makes a difference. The reality is that no matter what I do, Alzheimer's will win out at home.

There is nothing irrational about our fear. Our fear matches the facts. There is no cure for Alzheimer's and after 100 years, no disease-modifying therapeutics. What rescued earlier generations is that they died of other diseases first.

Is it any different for military caregivers, whose average age is 26, and who cope with the trauma and ravages of war that may cloud their lives for the foreseeable future? At the hospital, I approach a young man on a gurney, minus both arms and legs, being pushed by his wife, to thank them for service to our country and devotion to each other. My words seem wholly inadequate and their sacrifice unbearable.

Quite frankly, there is no time to see ourselves as victims. Even those who announce defiantly to the world that they have early-onset Alzheimer's are sooner or later marginalized professionally and socially. As advocates, we do battle with Medicaid and Medicare because no long-term care is covered unless you bankrupt

> "The greatest fear for many caregivers is that if we break down from physical or mental stress, there is no Plan B."

or divorce your spouse. We speak out for women who are two-thirds the victims and two-thirds the caregivers. Through the pain of our lived experiences, we form advocacy networks for African American and Latino minorities who will be the new majority of the future and reach out to work with the military on the needs of veterans now living with Alzheimer's and dementia.

I worry that people will be offended by my honesty about this disease. I don't think I have done anything that other caregivers haven't done for family and friends they love—though perhaps I have done it longer. But I claim no special expertise, and I refuse to pretend that my way is the right way.

When friends and family demand to know if my husband would have done the same for me, I can never easily answer them. Who among us can know with certainty how we will act until we are in the middle of things? I imagine he would have done whatever he could to get me the best medical attention and put me into the right pharmaceutical trials. But would he have abandoned his career to take care of me, bathe me, diaper me, dress me, feed me, cater to my every demand and personal need? I doubt it, nor quite frankly, would I want it. The real question isn't what Harvey might have done. It is: what I do I feel compelled to do as a loving and responsible human being?

Unfortunately, there are no road maps for survival. And that is how days slip into months, and months into years. I suffer no guilt, but that sensibility comes at an exorbitant personal price. Friends tried to rescue me, but I was too numb to hear and tired of defending my decision. Is it too late?

When I look in the mirror, I see only exhaustion and more than two decades lost. After all that has happened, and given the unknowns that lie ahead, I am still not sure that I could, or even would, have done things any differently.

Objectively, we are all at risk and potential victims—first, of the mind-wasting cruelty of the disease itself and, second, of societal failure to adequately respond to the breadth of the global Alzheimer's crisis. We are forced into a de facto moral dilemma "to care or not to care." Personally, it feels out of character and self-defeating for me to openly declare "moral injury," but I will own being a victim because I have chosen to be an advocate and that has made me fearless. ★

MERYL COMER *is president of the Geoffrey Beene Foundation Alzheimer's Initiative and co-founder of WomenAgainstAlzheimer's.*

CARRYING OUR BROTHERS TO SAFETY

MICHAEL DESMOND

I discovered the concept of moral injury two years ago. Through my military network I was forwarded an article by *Washington Post* staff writer Thomas Gibbons-Neff titled, "Haunted by Their Decisions in War." At the time, I was finishing my bachelor's degree in Public Health at DePaul University. The entire focus of my academic work after leaving the Marine Corps in 2012 had been focused on understanding the mental health disparities in the U.S. veteran population. Yet, somehow I had missed this piece of the puzzle.

I spent my last two years of high school conditioning myself for the Marine Corps, including running a minimum of two hours every day to Marine Corps cadence. I had one mantra in mind: "If your brother falls on the battlefield, will you be strong enough to carry him to safety?" I wanted to be prepared to fight the first moment I stepped into uniform.

On my first day out of intelligence school, when my Master Sergeant asked me if I wanted to go to Iraq as a combat reinforcement, I said yes before he could finish his question. But my experience integrating into an already-deployed unit in Iraq was not the greatest. No disrespect to the Marines I served with—it was more about me being a cocky kid from the Chicago suburbs who didn't have a problem speaking his mind.

Two months after returning from Iraq, I was already trying to go to Afghanistan. I hadn't been home to see my family yet, and the Master Sergeant who willfully sent me to Iraq now expressed concern. "Is everything okay?" he asked. "Are you in any kind of financial trouble? Are you having problems at home?" Despite his efforts, I found a workaround to get orders to an infantry battalion that was scheduled to deploy to Afghanistan.

It was June, and my November deployment turned into an April deployment, which meant spending almost a year in the field training for a possible mission in Afghanistan. We prepared for mountain and desert terrain, training in Sierra Nevada and the Bullion Mountains of California. I was ready to fight the Taliban but was about to face a struggle that would prove even more difficult.

I deployed into Helmand Province during President Obama's troop surge into Afghanistan, but the surge was accompanied by the planned withdrawal of U.S. forces. Forces in Iraq had already been scaled down considerably, and I was beginning to see the elements of terrorism I fought so hard against rise up again.

"We were only two months into the deployment when I lost a friend."

When I deployed to Afghanistan, I decided it would be my last tour. I had accomplished everything I set out to accomplish in the Marines, and I wanted to pursue college. My plan was to move back home and get a degree in classical Greek literature, because it had always been my favorite growing up, then law school after that. Much like I prepared for two years before joining the Marine Corps, I researched and worked myself back through works such as the *Iliad* and Plato's *The Republic*.

The allegory of the cave became the perfect metaphor for my service in Afghanistan. My commander-in-chief had already announced withdrawal. As an intelligence analyst, it was my job to think like a terrorist in order to catch a terrorist. When I thought about the withdrawal being four years away, how difficult security was to establish in our district, the rampant corruption in the Afghanistan government, and our own nation's inability to remain connected to the ongoing fight, it led me to feel that the days spent in that province would not be worth it. If I was a Taliban fighter who heard U.S. troops were leaving in a few years, I would just head out, stay with relatives in a bordering country, then come back in and fight once they left.

The Taliban fights with religious fervor but those in charge rationalize and strategize just like our sharpest military minds. They kept a presence in Afghanistan because a terrorist organization cannot pull back completely. That left me and the other 800 or so Marines tasked with securing the Garmsir District of Afghanistan with a tall order: establish security in the district while keeping a plan for sustainable transfers of power to our Afghan allies. That was a tough order considering we had been occupying Afghanistan for nine years at that point, and we were the only unit to secure our entire district since the first invasion.

But why is all of this significant? The point is that as a Marine I don't decide where I go or what I do. It is my sole purpose to live in complete dedication to the mission. In boot camp we are taught that the primary objective of Marine Corps leadership is mission accomplishment. I was 21 years old, reading Plato between 12-to-20 hour shifts managing drone coverage, and coordinating support for troops in direct combat. I didn't have a clear vision of how to accomplish the mission. That's when I abandoned the mission. I decided that the objective of the war, and what everyone in America was talking about, no longer mattered. We lost 14 warriors in Afghanistan. The casualties stacked up quickly in the beginning as we expanded south to secure our district as intended.

We were only two months into the deployment when I lost a friend I made on the way over. I just wanted to come home with as many of my fellow Marines as possible, which meant I had to prevent the enemy from successfully using roadside bombs and destroy as much of their network as possible. I succeeded to an extreme degree and ended up getting recognition for it and a meritorious promotion.

However, when I came back from Afghanistan, the sleepless nights started. Sometimes I would go three days without sleep. The post-traumatic stress was clearly evident, but I focused on training my Marines to take care of their brothers and volunteered to go on another deployment, extending my contract to do so. Why?

"Moral injury is not always about killing or being killed. For some of us, it is being placed in an environment where we will rely on one another in ways no one else will ever understand."

Because I couldn't live with the idea of staying behind while my Marines and the rest of my unit might be destined for combat. That deployment resulted in one of the worst depressions of my life because of one significant reason: I didn't deploy with the unit I went to Afghanistan with.

Combat experience is like an MBA in the infantry. You can move up in the ranks without it, but you should definitely have combat experience if you plan on becoming a leader. Warfighting is our business. When you spend more than a decade waging war it is expected that you find a way to combat. Otherwise it will be assumed you were avoiding it.

When we came back from Afghanistan our unit was stripped to the bare bones. Some Marines left after their first enlistment, others were transferred to other units in order to share our combat experience across the Corps. I spent ten months preparing for war with these Marines, then seven months more sharing the same losses and celebrating the same victories. Now, except for a small batch of us that remained for the last deployment, they were gone.

Moral injury is not always about killing or being killed. For some of us, it is being placed in an environment where we will rely on one another in ways no one else will ever understand. Yet, we were never given the time to work through the battles we brought home together. I don't know how many Marines my unit has lost since we got home. I stopped counting. I often wonder what difference could be made if we transitioned out of combat as meaningfully as we enter into it. ★

MICHAEL DESMOND *is a veteran support specialist at Volunteers of America Illinois' Moral Injury Repair Center.*

> "I often wonder what difference could be made if we transitioned out of combat as meaningfully as we enter into it."

LIMITS & LIFELINES

MONA HANFORD

As a child, I was taught to work hard and make wise choices. My grandparents were immigrants, and they believed in the American Dream. But they also had a deep faith. My grandfather was a priest in the Russian Orthodox Church, and I was taught that suffering was part of the human existence. Today, some refer to suffering as moral injury. But it does not matter what you call it, it hurts either way.

When I reached my personal limits, it hurt. Fortunately there were lifelines for me. Here is my story.

I met my husband Bill when I was a freshman in high school. We had a storybook romance and married the week after I graduated college. We had two children and, decades later, six grandchildren. We worked hard and had choices. So when Bill's leg, which had been troublesome ever since a childhood injury, became excruciatingly painful, we consulted an orthopedic surgeon at a well-known hospital. The surgeon suggested rebuilding the leg and replacing the knee. Trying to be cautious, we asked for a second opinion from the chairman of the orthopedic department at another medical school. When he agreed with our first doctor's recommendation, we proceeded with the surgery in 2001.

I will spare you the details, but after an 11-hour surgery to rebuild Bill's leg and knee, there were complications, then additional surgeries. His mind and body began to disintegrate, not improve. He had many dark days. How could I find cures? How could I reverse the downward spiral? Bill was disabled and depressed, and I felt like death was closing in. I called a priest. It was November 2004. The fire was roaring in the fireplace, and the hot chocolate was steaming in our mugs. The priest was patient and calm. Bill rallied as best he could and was upbeat. When I referred to his sadness and misery during the previous weeks, he simply said: "We all have bad days."

The priest gave me advice I never expected. "I am not worried about Bill, I am worried about you," she said. "This chapter can last a long time. The stress of caregiving can wear you down." She was right. I had reached my limits. I felt vulnerable and hopeless. My reservoir of resilience and patience was running dry. I was suffering moral injury. Her advice to me was simple but profound: "Put lifelines in place for yourself so you can be there to support Bill. You are only human, and your body and mind can suffer under stress." She anchored me with the Serenity Prayer. She reminded me that it was not all up to me, and she reminded me to trust in God.

An image from my childhood in New York City came to mind—the statue of Atlas that stands across the street from St. Patrick's Cathedral on Fifth Avenue. He's holding up the world. I decided then it was time for me to embrace just being a human being, not Atlas, not God. Thank goodness it is not up to me to hold up the world! Thank goodness there is a God with that responsibility! I was able to continue caring for Bill for seven more years knowing my limits and accepting the many lifelines we were given.

Bill continued to suffer, and he was afraid to die. He was very proficient at denial. He would insist he was fine, but he was suffering from his own moral injury. While it is true that he had disabling physical problems as well as dementia, the most painful injury was the injury to his soul. When he was five and his sister was three, they were guests at a neighbor's new pool and his sister drowned. No matter how many times he was told that at 5 years old and barely able to swim, he couldn't be responsible for

> "Her advice to me was simple but profound: 'Put lifelines in place for yourself so you can be there to support Bill.'"

saving her, he suffered quietly inside for decades. He grew up in a family where the coping mechanism was: stiff upper lip, nothing to be done, let's move on.

After years of quiet suffering, Bill found peace at last. His body finally gave out. In October 2012, he died peacefully at home under the care of hospice, with me and our dog by his bedside. Bill and I had come a long way together, and I am grateful for the many who helped us during the long, last chapter. ★

MONA HANFORD *is a teacher, nonprofit-activist, fundraiser, change agent, and end-of-life care activist.*

"I decided then it was time for me to embrace just being a human being, not Atlas, not God."

CHEYENNE WOMAN WARRIOR

NOREEN STARR

From the age of two, I lived in a white community and was kept from my Cheyenne family, language, culture, and ways. It took me many years to understand all that was missing inside my very core.

What was left after life in a small Midwestern town in Oklahoma wasn't much. I was reinjured over and over by the ones that should have protected me.

I have begun to learn about my own people from an adopted father, George Calls Him, a Ponca Minister. He taught me a lot and left me with many stories and much wisdom and enlightenment. There were many hours of sitting and talking and days of just being still and absorbing the whole environment of Native American living. It was the experience I had been craving all my life. I finally learned how to smile and actually laugh out loud. I felt accepted by a very large family, which took me in and breathed life into my very soul. I was finally welcome with my own kind. I was 15 years old. But I still was raw from the shame and humiliation and oppression I endured throughout my childhood. Then I became bitter and angry. Making no sense of any of it, I went day-to-day knowing I was still empty.

I joined the U.S. Army National Guard and went regular Army. While in the Army, I was raped and told, "it didn't happen" by my CO and my drill sergeants. Even worse, I was punished in the days that followed because I had to look at this man during drill and at the mess hall. I could always hear him because of this laugh. It was the same laugh I heard as he touched my skin and breathed in my face, his spit oozing down my neck and chest, the weight of his body on top of mine. I could only look up at the sun, barely seen through the murky, soupy sky as I prayed for my next breath.

But it was my own fault. I should have stayed on that bus. I should not have walked on that sidewalk. And I certainly should never have allowed it to happen. I am supposed to be able to protect myself, right? Oh well, *it never happened.* The people I should have been able to tell were the people punishing me and making it disappear. But I just learned to disappear instead, anytime I wanted. And I did, for years at a time.

I got out of the Army and, of course, married the most maniacal and cruel person I could attract. He locked me in a basement and beat and tortured me for two years. After losing a pregnancy due to being slammed down a flight of stairs, I got pregnant a second time. My daughter was born and was one week old when I took her and left. The last beating my husband gave me was severe. I waited until he fell asleep, then at my baby's 4 a.m. feeding I snuck out of the house with her and started banging on neighbors' doors screaming for help.

> "All that I thought was true was not."

Later, I was raped, again, at knife point when I was partying. Again, my fault; I'll just disappear. Now today I'm angry with myself because I failed to care for myself and my body.

I was an alcoholic and then a meth addict. In and out of treatment that never worked for me, I was spiritually dead. If I ever was not, I'm not sure I remember.

I went to doctors and therapists and took all the new nut pills. One combination finally worked. Again, all that I thought was true was not. And all that I felt in my own magical mind was a part of my past coming back to haunt me.

It wasn't until I was immersed in Cheyenne history in college that I understood the full meaning of genocide. By then I was in my 50s and raising two grandchildren. I did a lot of research on different subjects, such as suicide among kids, alcoholism, drug addiction, Native women in prisons, the uranium deposits and poisonings of specific reservations while mining for coal and gold, etc. One of the worst things I discovered was Indian Health Service's complicity with the U.S. federal government in using Indian people to test new drugs. Once approved by the American Medical Association, those same drugs were pulled from IHS pharmacies country-wide. There was a trial in the '80s dealing with sterilization using IUDs for birth control, which has never been made right as far as I know. Sterilization of a whole generation is unconscionable and could be considered genocide. There is still genocide today.

I cried for two semesters about all the horrors that took place and the reality of it took over; night terrors began to be an ongoing thing.

Now I am under the care of a doctor for military sexual trauma and post-traumatic stress disorder. Dealing with all of this is exhausting, but if not now, when? It's not going to just go away. I'm angry and terrified that it will break my mind. Nobody cared before, why would they care now? I just don't know.

It is my responsibility and honor to do for the defenseless and those who can't do for themselves. As a Cheyenne woman warrior, it is my duty to speak for all the women in military who have been violated by a fellow soldier and then by the very establishment for which our flag stands. I will use my voice.

Will I carry this silently? No, not anymore. Not today. And not for the rest of my life. ★

NORENE STARR *works for the Cheyenne/Arapaho people of Oklahoma as a resource manager in the executive office.*

"Dealing with all of this is exhausting, but if not now, when? It's not going to just go away."

MISSION: POSSIBLE

ORLANDO WARD

The day I looked around and realized I could either transform my life or die was the day I hit rock bottom. It was also the day I was reborn.

I traveled a long path to get to that point, including 17 years of alcohol and substance abuse and two years of homelessness while living in a "cardboard condo" on Skid Row in downtown Los Angeles. But on a day in the spring of 1999, I knew I had no choice but to get better or perish.

I remember talking to God as I was sitting on my cardboard, which I placed on top of pallets to provide protection from rats and other things crawling on the ground. Despite everything, I knew I had lived a privileged life in many ways, and I thanked Him for that. I also remember telling Him I couldn't do it anymore. I was so tired. I had resigned myself to dying in that place. But He had other plans. Ultimately so did I.

The life I was living was never the one I, or anyone who knew me, imagined. I grew up in a middle class neighborhood in LA, with loving parents. I became a basketball star in high school and was recruited by countless universities as graduation approached. I chose Stanford, where I could excel in my sport and my education. But then I injured my knee in my sophomore year and effectively put an end to any dream I had of heading to the NBA.

My injury also sparked an identity crisis. I had defined myself through basketball for so long that I no longer knew who I was without it. I no longer had an anchor.

"I had defined myself through basketball for so long that I no longer knew who I was without it."

Things stopped mattering. I was lost. I took up with the wrong people and began filling the hole in my identity with things that were self-destructive.

After I graduated from Stanford, things continued to go downhill. I started a career as a marketing representative for Xerox, and worked very hard, but I played very hard, too. Every day of work would segue into happy hour, often followed by happy night or happy weekend. Soon, my drinking and drug use were no longer recreational, they became the reasons I worked at all. I was no longer the person I was before. Not that I could see any of that.

My friends and family noticed the change, but I would dismiss their concerns. *Clearly, they're the ones with the problem*, I thought. *I got this. You guys need to lighten up.* But my life was slipping away. My friends started to cut me off. They got tired of the excuses, tired of the requests for money. Again and again, I let those closest to me down, especially my family. I remember calling my mom one day and telling her some story about why I needed money again. She stopped me and said: "Orlando, I don't know what you're doing, but I didn't raise you this way. I can't help." Then she hung up.

With no money and no support system left, I ended up on the streets. Someone who has never been to Skid Row will have a difficult time imagining it. Block after block, forgotten people live on the streets, in tents on the sidewalk, any place there's room—the injured, the mentally ill, the addicted, the elderly, people of all different ages and backgrounds living side by side. Many people live on Skid Row for years, in conditions most Americans think can only be found in the developing world. Shelters and social service agencies fill the neighborhood, but they can only do so much given the demand. And for those like me, battling addiction and inner demons, attempts to help fall on deaf ears until we are willing and able to make changes inside ourselves. Skid Row was never a place I ever expected to find myself, but by the time I realized just how low I had gotten, it was too late.

After two years on Skid Row and surrendering myself to what I thought was my fate, I found myself at the Midnight Mission—a shelter on the Row that helps people overcome the problems that led them to homelessness. My first job in

> "Skid Row was never a place I ever expected to find myself, but by the time I realized just how low I had gotten, it was too late."

many years was working part-time in the Mission's kitchen. It wasn't the work I went to Stanford to do, but it was my first step back to stability and self-sufficiency. When the staff saw promise in me and started increasing my levels of responsibility, a shift began to occur inside me. I started to see that the life I had been living was unacceptable.

I was able to gain control over my addictions, graduate from the Mission's programs and return to a productive professional life. It was a transformation I thought, at one point, was impossible. My productivity did not mean my time at the Mission was over. I took a job working at the Mission full-time, using my own experiences to show others that their lives have no limits. I eventually worked my way up to vice president of operations. I had discovered a new purpose in life, one much grander than basketball.

I've since moved on from the Midnight Mission, but not my new calling. Several years ago, I began work as executive vice president of external affairs at Volunteers of America Greater Los Angeles, another human-service organization with a major presence on Skid Row. I now work with the media, donors, foundations, and many others, to communicate the work of our organization and tell the stories of those we serve. I also share my own story.

I often act as a liaison between Volunteers of America and those still living on the streets. In this new role, my demons, which once seemed like a curse, have become a blessing. I wouldn't be where I am today without my experience living on the streets. Those memories have become the tools of my trade. They allow me to help others, relate to how they are feeling, and let them know there is a way out.

Unlike most people who avoid Skid Row, I am comfortable being there. While it hurts to see the suffering, my own experiences there make me feel empowered to help. Sometimes I'll run into friends still living there. "You're doing well," they'll say. "One day I'll be there, too." Hearing those words gives me a purpose and a grounding that I value immensely.

I still feel guilt and shame over the relationships I lost during my years of addiction. The worst are my feelings about the way I treated my parents. Fortunately, as the result of a great deal of work, I was able to rebuild my

"Someone who has never been to Skid Row will have a difficult time imagining it."

relationship with my mother and father. In the process, I learned how much they mean to me and how important my presence is in their lives. I also started giving back to my mother after asking so much of her in years past. A while back, when my dad had a mild stroke, I was the first person they called. They rely on me now. But I think their reliance and trust does more for me than it does for them.

God is not done with me yet, and I know there is much more for me to do. ★

ORLANDO WARD *is executive vice president of external affairs at Volunteers of America Greater Los Angeles.*

"I wouldn't be where I am today without my experience living on the streets. Those memories have become the tools of my trade."

GUIDED FORWARD

ORSON BUCKMIRE

I was born and raised in Boston, Massachusetts and lived there most of my life. I joined the Army while I was in college because I was ready to go beyond the borders of Massachusetts and experience what life had to offer.

I enlisted in March of 1998 and shipped out in April. I was 19 years old. My first assignment was working as a cook in a duty station in Seoul, Korea. There was some culture shock, but I found Seoul to be a lot like New York. I used my free time to explore, getting to know my surroundings and the culture. The experience gave me exactly what I was looking for from my enlistment.

After two years in Korea, I returned stateside to Fort Stewart, Georgia. I was with an infantry unit, so we spent a lot of time in the field and did a lot of training.

On the morning that everything changed, I was in my room getting ready for my shift. I put on the TV, and the first tower had already been hit. I thought to myself, *why are they always trying to blow up New York in every movie?* I changed the channel and saw the same picture on every station. I thought something wrong with my TV. Then it dawned on me.

This is real. This is really happening.

Seconds later, my platoon sergeant called me and told me to get downstairs with all my stuff. My unit was put on alert until we got orders. From that day forward everything ramped up across the military. Everyone knew we were about to go to war, we just didn't know where.

Shortly after 9/11, my initial contract came up for renewal. I felt there were too many things in the army I needed to do, so I looked into my options and decided to become a medic. After four months of training, I went back to Korea for a third year.

This time I didn't land in a cushy post like Seoul, I landed in the Demilitarized Zone (DMZ), a mile away from North Korea. Tensions were especially high during that period, but being that close to the enemy turned out to be the best year of training I ever received. The high pressure and seriousness of the situation fine-tuned my skills and focus as a medic. As a result, my platoon and I made a lot of good things happen.

After the DMZ post, I went to Fort Campbell in Clarksville, Tennessee where I was afforded the opportunity to serve in a unit with heavy combat experience. I was promoted to sergeant, and we were deployed to Iraq in December 2004.

We were deployed from 2004 to 2005, one of the bloodiest years the U.S. experienced while in the Middle East. The farther south of Iraq, the safer it was, but there was limited medical support. A lot of people were running away from the violence and moving into rural areas—that's where I started. As the deployment wore on, I was tasked to head to Baghdad where I spent the last six or seven months of my time.

As medics we not only take care of our own service members, we have to take care of prisoners of war. In some cases, it felt like we were treating the prisoners better than our own men, if only because the higher-ups wanted to get our enemies well so we could pump them for information.

Around this time, Saddam Hussein was caught and preparing to stand trial. We treated him at our Combat Support Hospital in Baghdad, and I was responsible for making his file. I was in the same room with him only once and it felt like I was standing with the devil. This man was responsible for thousands of deaths, and he was sitting in front of me trying to flirt with a nurse—reciting poetry to her—while I put his file together. In terms of the banality of evil, that moment put a lot into perspective for me—we were fighting madmen.

The capture of Saddam wasn't particularly meaningful for those of us fighting. We knew we were still going to be there whether he was captured or not. His detainment wouldn't change the fact that we went to sleep to the sounds of gunfire every night. I didn't get a whole lot of sleep when I was in Bagdad because the nights were just as eventful as the days. The darkness

"We were deployed from 2004 to 2005, one of the bloodiest years the U.S. experienced while in the Middle East."

and stillness of the night made everything feel more real. It made movies and TV shows that depict war look superficial. To witness war in person—to smell it, hear it, live with it—is something entirely different. Something awful.

My faith was also tested. I witnessed countless deaths and dismemberments and saw mass casualties every day. Experiencing this on a daily basis made me wonder, *what are we here for? Why is this kid's arm blown off? Why does this female service member have shrapnel in her brain? Where's the rest of this guy's face? Why are we here?*

I became disillusioned. I started questioning the purpose of all the fighting. *Where were these weapons of mass destruction, and why are we in Iraq when the people who hijacked the planes on 9/11 did not come from Iraq?* There were no good answers to those questions, and I knew it.

After completing that year, I got out of the military. But leaving wasn't my intention. I tried to get re-classed as an X-ray technician, but it didn't work out and I felt slighted. When an experienced serviceman offers to stay in, it's considered a golden egg among Army brass. But they dropped the ball administratively and, with all my other frustrations compounding, I officially got out in January 2006.

My first year as a civilian was turbulent. I was living in Atlanta, going through a divorce and suffering from post-traumatic stress disorder. I went back to Boston briefly, connected with the VA and got some help for my PTSD, which also helped me cope with being back in the civilian sector.

A brief ray of hope shined when I was afforded an opportunity to work in Texas. I moved there, but the job didn't work out. The experience left me burned-out and feeling like civilian life wasn't going to work for me. I resorted to doing everything I could to get back into the military, but I couldn't seem to make that work either.

In spite of the strain my morale was under, I clung to the idea that everything happens for a reason. I knew, deep down, there was something important for me to do and experience in the civilian sector. I put my faith in the idea that a higher power would guide me forward.

And it did.

Not long after I moved to Texas, things started turning around. I met the person who would become the mother of my child, and I found a job on the base where she

> "To witness war in person—to smell it, hear it, live with it—is something entirely different. Something awful."

was stationed. I worked at an urgent care facility, treating the children of military families. It was an enriching new challenge that reminded me of why I became a medical professional in the first place.

After that job ended, I decided to move back to Boston. I touched down in Massachusetts without housing, employment, or any other resources in place. Despite having so little to fall back on, I felt there was a reason I was coming back to Boston, I just didn't know what it was.

While looking for housing and employment, I ran across Volunteers of America. They helped me get back on my feet and prepare to go back to school. As fall approached, Volunteers of America Massachusetts informed me of an internal job posting within the Supportive Services for Veterans and encouraged me to apply. Once I discovered the job was helping homeless people off the streets and connecting them with employment, I realized I had found my reason to return to Boston. To my delight, I got the job.

Since 2015 I've been doing case management and outreach for Volunteers of America. My military experience enriches the work I do by helping me develop deeper connections with veterans who have gone through struggles similar to mine. What we do—helping struggling veterans find meaningful jobs and places of their own—illustrates how the momentum of hope is unlimited.

For that reason, the advice I give veterans trying to find their way back from a path of trauma and disillusionment is this: get help right away, stay focused, and don't lose faith that the direction you're heading toward is the right one. That faith makes all the difference. ★

ORSON BUCKMIRE *is case manager/outreach coordinator with Volunteers of America Massachusetts' Veterans Employment Network. His story was told to Isaac Oden of Volunteers of America Massachusetts.*

"What we do—helping struggling veterans find meaningful jobs and places of their own—illustrates how the momentum of hope is unlimited."

FINDING A WAY FORWARD

ROBERT HOPPER

When I brought my mother, Mildred, back to Illinois from Florida in December 2008, I was well aware that she would require assistance with every facet of her life.

My father, Bill, passed away in May 2002, and my mother decided to stay in the home they had moved into the month before he died. She was blessed to have a good network of neighbors and friends, which enabled her to do well for the first couple of years in spite of health problems, including blindness in one eye and a series of ministrokes.

However, by the end of 2006, her physician recommended I consider other housing options. In addition to the ministrokes, she was also having recurring urinary tract infections, which are far more serious than most people realize. Symptoms can include extreme confusion, hallucinations, and extreme weakness that can result in the person being bedridden or susceptible to falls. My mother was having all of those symptoms. She was also diagnosed with mild dementia. Her doctor told me that more serious complications were possible if she did not have a more structured living arrangement. I started to talk with her about moving.

My wife and I have a one-bedroom condominium unit in Illinois; it's on the third floor of a building without an elevator. In previous years when my mother came to visit, she was able to make it up and down the stairs once a day. She could no longer manage that, so I started to look for senior housing for her. The closest facility where she could have a studio apartment and keep her small dog (the dog my father bought her before he died) was 40 minutes from our home.

In November 2008, I flew to Florida to begin moving my mother to Illinois. We had to put her home on the market, pack up all of her belongings, and ship most of the boxes to my cousin's home until I could get a storage locker for her. Then I rented a large SUV and drove her and her dog to Illinois. I timed the travel—one night, two days—to arrive in the morning so she could get into her new apartment by the end of the day.

Over the next seven years, my mother had ups and downs, physically, emotionally, and spiritually. Although she lived in an assisted-care facility that provided a moderate level of support and care, I took care of her laundry, walked her dog, managed her finances, took her to her medical appointments, took her to get her hair and nails done, and spent time just visiting with her. On average, I visited her three-to-four nights each week and once over the weekend.

In addition to the time spent with her, I spent 90 minutes driving to-and-from wherever she was at the time—her apartment, the hospital, and finally the nursing and rehabilitation facility. Sometimes I spent more time driving than I did visiting, but as she declined, especially during her last two years, if I didn't show up she would become confused and, sometimes, scared and angry. I also couldn't hold the facilities accountable for the quality of care she received if I didn't visit.

Thankfully my wife helped out, and my mother appreciated when she accompanied me during visits and outings. My daughter also helped out and often visited her grandmother after work, especially on the nights when I did not because of fatigue or bad weather. The bond between them became so strong, whereas before the relationship it had been quite strained. That was truly a gift for both of them, and a great help to me.

My mother made a few new friends, but it was difficult for her. She had hearing aids but didn't like to wear them and wasn't able to put them in herself so she often went without them. In the spring of 2014, we had to have her dog put down. It was devastating for her.

In her last two years, she had to move to a nursing and rehab center, which meant sharing a room. She had good roommates, but the loss of privacy and her declining

"I often felt torn by feelings of selfishness and obligation, and I struggled with emotional and physical fatigue and the demands of my work."

sensory and cognitive functioning led to bouts of depression and withdrawal. Though she had fewer urinary tract infections, when she did have them it required hospitalization and resulted in subsequent declines in functioning.

Her ability to engage in conversation and recreational activities became more and more impaired as her cognitive functioning declined and her depression continued. This was the most emotionally challenging period of my caregiving. While I understood her inability to engage in meaningful, give-and-take conversation, I felt angry, frustrated, and often reluctant to visit because of the mostly one-sided nature of our interactions. There were many times that I didn't want to visit her, and I delayed my arrival or shortened my visits because I just wanted to do something for myself. My family, friends, and my spiritual father provided much needed encouragement over the years as I cared for my mother because the challenges were real and often overwhelming. And yet, there were times I wished I were completely unknown and disconnected from all those around me. I thought the isolation would be a refuge and what I deserved for my lack of patience, consistent love, and understanding for my mother and what she was going through.

There were times when I hurt my mother's feelings, such as when I expressed my frustration with her refusal to ask for help from the nurses' aides and staff because she didn't want to bother anyone or make things difficult for me. Managing her bank account and trust, paying her bills, and driving to visit her seemed to take so much of my time that I felt like I was on a treadmill when I wasn't at work.

But there were times of great joy and fun, too, especially when my wife and I would bring our grandson to visit and play cards with his great grandmother, or when we would go out to breakfast and take her to get her nails done. But I often felt torn by feelings of selfishness and obligation, and I struggled with emotional and physical fatigue and the demands of my work. There were countless times when I wanted to turn over all the responsibilities to someone else and restrict my visits to once a week.

It has been more than two years since my mother passed away. I believe I did the best I could under the circumstances, but sometimes I feel like I failed to be the son and caregiver my mother needed and deserved. Today, I can live with that without allowing it to take me down. One day at a time is the way forward. ★

ROBERT HOPPER *is the employment service coordinator for Volunteers of America Illinois' True North Project.*

I SURVIVED

SHARMIN PRINCE

Sharmin Prince is the fifth of six children and was the last child in her family until 1971. She was fearless and smart and loved music so much that whenever she heard it she danced. When she performed in concerts with her kindergarten class, she was always in the front row. Sharmin was advanced for her age and very popular in the neighborhood. Her mother was an employee of the public hospital and was also very popular. Sharmin was a mommy's girl.

Sharmin's grandmother and her mother's siblings lived in a rural area. When they came into the city, they visited Sharmin and her family and often stayed overnight. The house was already overcrowded, but Sharmin's mother welcomed her family whenever they came; her youngest brother did not have a job and sometimes stayed for weeks on end.

In 1971, when Sharmin was five years old, that uncle came for a visit. As she slept on the bed he raped her, then left her crying. Soon after she became a target for the Harris brothers. The boys were much older than her, and four of the six abused her. All of this occurred in the same year, but Sharmin did not tell anyone. Her academic abilities started to decline. She began acting out by fighting. She was very angry. Sharmin's mother was a single parent and had no idea her daughter was a school-yard bully. Sharmin fought one of her classmates four times one week and kept it a secret from her mother and siblings. She was skilled at carrying secrets. But she knew how to take abuse; she got whipped in school and at home.

Sharmin witnessed a lot of violence in her neighborhood between the ages of ten and fifteen. During one incident, a woman went to the market and returned home later than expected so her husband broke a bottle across her head and stabbed her several times while Sharmin watched. Sharmin witnessed this man abuse this woman on several occasions and endured a high level of vicarious trauma in the process.

When Sharmin entered adolescence, she began directing her anger toward boys. At school and in her neighborhood, Sharmin said things she knew the boys wouldn't like just to get into fights with them. Many feared her. Bullying gave her a sense of control and power.

"But she knew how to take abuse; she got whipped in school and at home."

Sharmin was transferred to a prestigious high school and got into a fight the first week. This time, however, Sharmin was not the bully—the girl she was fighting with had been bullied in primary school. When Sharmin's name was announced over the loudspeaker it embarrassed her. She had to get her mother from work before being readmitted to the school.

Not surprisingly, Sharmin entered into an abusive relationship for a number of years. One night she retaliated and cut her abuser several times. Another time, he hit her and she swung a four-by-six plank to hit him back but broke a piece of furniture instead.

The first time Sharmin told anyone about being sexually abused she was twenty-five years old living in French Guyana. She was an avid and unapologetic pot smoker. A man she was dating shot at her and she laughed while telling him he was shooting at her feet while her body was exposed. Her friends intervened.

Soon after, Sharmin made a 180-degree turn and became a devout Christian. She enrolled in a one-year college and graduated with distinction. She then pursued a degree in social work at the University of Guyana and also graduated with distinction. She started working toward a Bachelor of Science degree but migrated to the United States before completion.

One year after migrating to the U.S., Sharmin entered the United States Army and successfully completed basic training. But she was falling apart emotionally and did not know why. Vicarious trauma and post-traumatic stress disorder were things never spoken about, so she did not understand what was happening to her. She began to have flashbacks about the abuse she endured and the violence she witnessed, which resulted in a discharge from the Army after a year. Sharmin has since been diagnosed with PTSD. This is only half of her story. ★

SHARMIN PRINCE *is a program director for Volunteers of America-Greater New York.*

"Vicarious trauma and post-traumatic stress disorder were things never spoken about, so she did not understand what was happening to her."

STRIVING FOR BALANCE

SHELA WEBB

My injuries date back to when I was very young. They began at age three and continued until I was 12, all inflicted by my father. I'm just beginning to deal with the repercussions because I thought I'd gotten past everything that happened. No therapist had ever put the pieces together until now. My history of injury is probably the reason for my many failed relationships, my inability to form friendships, my lack of trust in some cases and trusting too much in others. It's also the reason I keep everyone at a distance.

My parents divorced when I was six, and I watched my mother drink a lot and fall in-and-out of love just as often. I saw my father in the summers and lived with him in Alaska during my 5th grade year. He would molest me almost daily after becoming too drunk to realize what he was doing. The father of my best friend at the time would also attempt to molest me but stopped at his daughter's request; my friend and I were both 11.

I moved around often as a kid and, subsequently, many more times while I served 22 years in the military—43 addresses in 46 years of living. I thought the military would be my sanctuary, a place where I could be myself and do the things I longed to do:

mechanics, serve my country, see the world. But I was injured again, and on more than one occasion.

The biggest injury came very early in my career. The last question on my military contract asked if I was homosexual or had ever engaged in homosexual activities. I marked NO. It was a lie that would haunt me my entire career. The truth was that I was a lesbian and had been as far back as my memory allowed.

That lie cost me my identity for the better part of my adult life. It forced me to be silent and to deny my true self and those I loved. I was never able to share my life with a partner, to have them greet me at the pier when my ship pulled in, or to invite them to work functions. I feared daily that I would be found out and would lose my career. It was painful.

The Don't Ask, Don't Tell (DADT) movement finally caught up with me during my initial enlistment. I was summoned to courts-martial for allegedly sexually harassing a woman who was older and who held a higher rank than me. My reenlistment and a promotion were put on hold as I began the biggest battle of my life: to falsely prove I was not gay in order to save my career.

Courts-martial kicked the case back to my squadron because nobody wanted to touch such a sensitive topic. The day before my administrative separation board was to be held, homosexuality was added to my charges and the focus of the case shifted.

I was found not guilty of the charge of sexual harassment, but guilty of the charge of being gay. Despite the shining character references my superiors supplied, the board members recommended an honorable discharge and sent me on my way.

My career was placed on hold, and I was tasked with mundane jobs on the base while my senators and congressman appealed the decision to the Department of Defense and the Secretary of the Navy. I was finally allowed to reenlist after having extended my term every month for four months, but I realized I needed to protect myself. So, I married a male friend who understood my dilemma.

I was sexually harassed daily throughout my career and, on three separate occasions, sexually assaulted by male coworkers after I passed out from too much drinking. I've been a fighter all my life and never complained about much, so I never said anything. I also feared the arguments against having women in the military would be proven correct if anyone found out what was going on. I'd recently played a part in introducing women on combat ships and in other combat roles in different branches, and I was excited to be involved in that history.

"He would molest me almost daily after becoming too drunk to realize what he was doing."

I left the Navy after 10 years of being a jet mechanic, two stints in rehab for alcohol, eight failed relationships, three rapes, one possible miscarriage, six deployments, four units, 10 different addresses, a fake marriage, and a partridge in a pear tree! Next, I headed to the Army to become a counselor so I could help others.

I trained to be a Combat Medic/Mental Health Specialist and Career Counselor and, soon after, was deployed to Iraq during the initial invasion. I witnessed more harassment, pain, and misery there and often felt that military women were there as eye candy for the "boys." But just as I did in the Navy, I tried to fit in and be one of the guys.

I was alone and lonely and, again, unable to talk about my life and my partner and about how much I missed her. Instead, I had to use my fake marriage as a cover. I served in five units, lived in five states, endured one long deployment, five failed relationships, one real marriage (after gay marriages were allowed), one fake divorce, one real divorce, lost an eight-year run at sobriety (followed by another six-year run), earned a bachelor's degree, and saw the repeal of DADT, which somehow angered me.

After 22 years of service, I was retired due to a bad back. Had the military not retired me I would probably still be there, and I don't know why that is. I feel like I don't belong anywhere else, and maybe abuse is all I'll ever know. I have finally been diagnosed with post-traumatic stress disorder and military sexual trauma and have joined a therapy group to examine my injuries and attempt to make repairs.

My entire life has been spent living within extremes: too much bad and too little good. I am slowly starting to find the middle where there is calm. ★

SHELA WEBB *is a case manager with Volunteers of America Northern California and Northern Nevada.*

> "I feel like I don't belong anywhere else, and maybe abuse is all I'll ever know."

"My entire life has
been spent living
within extremes:
too much bad
and too little good."

FERGUSON & THE SPIRIT OF ST. LOUIS

Soul Trauma and Civic Imagination

STARSKY D. WILSON

Every city has a soul: a unique personality, an ethical identity, an animating spirit. In the language of some faith traditions (including my own) the soul is alternatively spoken of as the heart and the seat of one's will. In 2014, matters of the heart and soul for the people of St. Louis captured the world's imagination.

Our region celebrates its founding as February 14, 1764, when Pierre Laclède and Auguste Chouteau established the settlement of St. Louis. In 2014, a community-wide celebration of a milestone anniversary (#StL250) was in full swing, and I served on the steering committee. The festivities began on Valentine's weekend with a "Burning Love" party in Forest Park, our city's crown jewel. A virtual bakery of commissioned birthday cake statues littered the local landscape, marking historical landmarks and cultural institutions.

The year was off to a great start. We were successfully celebrating the best of our civic identity, the soul of the city. In June, one of the defining characteristics of our self-image was acknowledged nationally when Charity Navigator named us "Most Charitable Region" in their annual metropolitan market survey. With a United Way campaign outpacing our population size, a five-star Urban League affiliate leading its peers, and well-endowed institutions of higher learning, such as Washington

University in St. Louis, our philanthropy has always been a source of pride. Indeed, it was the philanthropy of a small group of St. Louisans that wrote us into the history books in a moment that captured the imagination of the world.

In 1927, Charles Lindbergh made the first solo, non-stop transatlantic flight from Long Island, New York to Paris, France. Lindbergh was originally from Detroit, and later a resident of New Jersey and England, and his famous aircraft, which now greets visitors at the National Air and Space Museum in Washington, DC, was named *The Spirit of St. Louis* in honor of the benefactors who paid for it. The charitable spirit of a few of our citizens carried the city into a moment that sparked international interest, investment, and pursuit of the wild blue yonder.

If nothing else, the spirit of the city of St. Louis is charitable, philanthropic, and caring. This is why the killing of Michael Brown, Jr. on August 9, 2014, in Ferguson, Missouri, was so painful for many. The city of Ferguson only makes up six square miles and 20,000 people in the St. Louis metropolitan area, but what took place on August 9 initiated a continuum of collective suffering and questioning that touched the hearts of every citizen and the soul of the entire region.

> "This is the stuff of soul trauma, an example of mass moral injury."

Consider these juxtapositions: the image of this young, black teenager expiring for four hours in the street, while birthday cakes marked our "important" corners. The idea that one called to public service took his life, as we celebrated commitment to public benefit. The fact that "Mike Mike" had just finished high school, while we took pride in the resources of our colleges. The reality that our social programs could not save him, as we prepared to launch our annual workplace campaigns. The picture of his crying mother restrained by yellow crime scene tape a few miles from Lindbergh Boulevard, named for the famed aviator.

This is the stuff of soul trauma, an example of mass moral injury. The very spirit of St. Louis came into question.

Were we who we said—or believed—we were? Do the actions of public servants say more about who we are than the checks we write? Are the choices of Officer Darren Wilson, the refusal of county prosecutor Robert McCullough to pursue charges against him, and a history of racial fragmentation through policymaking more reflective of the spirit of St. Louis? Was the uprising of a youth-led, black-led and multi-racial coalition calling for police reform a more appropriate acknowledgement of our milestone anniversary?

In late August that year, while running errands after picking up my sons from school, I tried to keep up with the shifting narrative about the uprising through radio news. My son, Starsky II, all of nine years old at the time, began to express symptoms of injury. From the backseat of the car he said, "Dad, every time I hear about Michael Brown my stomach starts to hurt." Challenged by the statement, I gave him permission to leave any room where the discussion was happening and to remind me that I need to monitor myself on the topic as well.

Of course, his pain could have been the fear and anxiety of a young, black boy wondering if what happened to Michael Brown would ever happen to him. He could have been diagnosed with toxic stress. Then again, as a child of two parents who are human-service professionals, a young person raised in a church where voluntarism for community uplift is encouraged, and a good student in a public, magnet school where he learned a history of American exceptionalism, it seemed he was presenting the signs of our entire community's internal conflict. His stomachache was a sign of guilt and grief because he thought we were better than this. He was not alone.

In November, Missouri's governor, Jeremiah Nixon, asked me to co-chair the Ferguson Commission—a group of 16 citizens empowered to study the underlying issues exposed by Michael Brown's death and to make public policy recommendations to build a stronger, fairer, and more inclusive community. The commission held public meetings for more than a year and listened to citizen-experts in life experience, academic credential, and policymaking. In four of the meetings, we polled the group about trauma and toxic stress.[1]

The folks in our meetings hurt like little Starsky. On average, 70% of attendees had experienced trauma and toxic stress and 72% believed the community in which they lived suffered trauma. The traumatic potential of racism was not lost on them. On average, 98% of respondents believed someone can be traumatized by racism and 55% had experienced trauma due to racism themselves.

Frankly, by the time we got to the real-time polling in those 2015 meetings, we knew what they would tell us. We heard tear-filled testimony about economic inequity from a young woman who worked a double shift at a fast food restaurant to buy diapers for her child. We heard a high school senior who called for cultural competence in the classroom based upon the teacher who comforted him through the

1   https://forwardthroughferguson.org/
report/executive-summary/ accessed
February 22, 2018.

loss of his mother. In both instances, I saw well-positioned business leaders charitably respond to these individual stories behind the scenes. Perhaps, though, these were insufficient efforts and attempts to assuage the internal trauma of coming face-to-face with the impact of their support of systems that produce results misaligned with their stated values.

While many questions and concerns were addressed through the Commission's meetings, the most critical one was underlying and not explicitly stated: How might we become the people we've already been saying we are? It seemed to me, if a nostalgic civic imagination (with a few glaring gaps) could get us here, an inclusive, visionary process of collective imagining might get us out.

Beyond the stated charge of Executive Order 14–15, which established the Ferguson Commission, this was our real work: to steward a process of cultivating civic imagination in response to the pain of communal soul trauma. Ultimately, the 3,000 people who worked through their own pain in this effort, articulated a vision of racial equity as their eschatological hope.

Hopefully, our pain and process can be instructive for the nation. Situated in the heart [read "soul"] of America, St. Louis held a high sense of self, reflective and intertwined with that of the nation. When Alexis de Tocqueville traveled the United States in the 1830s, he took note of the voluntary associations and spirit of philanthropy in his book, *Democracy in America*. With the realities of this moment, our well-being may be well served by a period of soul searching and a common space to imagine. ★

REV. STARSKY WILSON *is pastor of Saint John's Church (The Beloved Community) and president and CEO of Deaconess Foundation. He formerly led the Ferguson Commission.*

"With the realities of this moment, our well-being may be well served by a period of soul searching and a common space to imagine."

PULLING THE CURTAIN

STUART FRANKLIN

I served in the Army from June 1977 to August 1986. I was a Behavioral Science specialist, but I had many different titles. What I usually tell people is that I was the non-commissioned officer in charge of the Department of Psychology and Neurology for the Womack Army Hospital in Fort Bragg, North Carolina.

But I didn't start out there. My first duty assignment in the Army was supposed to be Hawaii, but I turned it down to go to Germany. I had to bribe the girl who worked in the assignment department with $130 and a case of Pampers to get her to change my papers. It was one the best decisions I ever made.

I consider my abilities to read, write, and truly understand German some of my greatest achievements. These skills helped me teach the soldiers in my care how to better adapt to the country and how to understand German culture, which can be polarizing.

Back then people would say to me, "You're not married, you have no kids, what are your priorities?" I would tell them I was married to my job. My ex-girlfriend would beg me to stay at home when duty called. I'd always answer her the same way: "I have troops that need me."

Military recognition was insignificant to me and other relationships always took a backseat. My troops always took first priority, and my focus was helping them. That was the foundation of my beliefs and values when serving my country. It informed my every decision and gave my life meaning.

Those values would be shaken in the summer of 1986, when I had to abandon my military career because my twin sister was murdered. The loss was, and still is, too shocking and tragic to describe.

I never imagined that by serving my country I would leave my loved ones vulnerable to this sort of tragedy. I internalized that thought regardless of how irrational it was. The pain, the guilt, and the conflict of leaving one life behind to try to pick up the pieces of another would follow me for years to come. I had to grapple with the loss of my sister as well as the loss of what I thought was my life's meaning.

In the wake of the tragedy, I had to set my feelings aside. There was no adjustment period for change. I never asked the VA for help. I had new responsibilities and had to move forward. I returned home to New York to take care of my niece and my mother. That became my new objective as I began a civilian life.

I immediately went out to find work and began employment with a non-profit program that helped the developmentally disabled. Giving back to others while supporting my family seemed like the perfect way to stay ahead of the trauma I experienced. For a while, it seemed to work.

I went from being the organization's weekend respite to becoming a full-time staff member, then program manager, then program director. Eventually, I became the CEO of the organization. With this change came added stress. The new stress combined with my residual feelings of loss and guilt brought me to yet another internal struggle.

When you're in charge of so much and dealing with so many important, prominent people, you learn to go with the flow. Telling myself I was doing a service to my organization, my family and myself, I tried to enhance my focus with the use of substances, mainly cocaine. Cocaine was part of the CEO lifestyle and was culturally acceptable behind closed doors. It was easy to get swept up in it, and my life became like something out of a bad Martin Scorsese movie. The substances made my guilt and pain even worse.

Yet I did not seek help for my issues. I suppose I lost faith in what I was doing, why I was doing it, and for whom I was doing it. I tried to kill myself three separate

"My troops always took first priority, and my focus was helping them."

times in the years that followed. Each time God gave me another chance. In 2010, He brought me to a final crossroads.

That was the year I found out I had a 14-year-old son living in Gardner, Massachusetts. I was 50 years old and, as you can imagine, the revelation blew my mind. After we met he asked if he could take my last name. He was a blessing during a dark time.

I moved to Massachusetts to be with by son. Reconnecting with him was one of the most amazing experiences of my life. But shortly after receiving this blessing, my life was interrupted again.

One evening, while walking home, I was run down by a hit-and-run driver. In the aftermath, I went 15 minutes without oxygen to the brain and lost nine months of my life to a coma.

During this time, my family rallied behind me. My brother, niece, and mother stayed by my side. They had faith that God would guide me out of my coma. There's a video they took soon after my accident where they're trying to wake me up. My brother keeps saying, "Stuart, pull the curtain. Stuart. Pull the curtain." Seeing the footage, and everything I went through with my family by my side giving me their love and support, overwhelms me to the point of tears—tears of joy and of sadness. My emotions defy description.

I consider myself lucky to be able to experience these feelings now. I consider myself lucky that God gave me the strength to finally pull the curtain on my birthday. My family recorded that moment on video, too. In the footage, my brother says, "You think you're special, huh?" I reply with the one word: "Very."

I still feel that way. God didn't have to let me stay here. But He had other plans.

After waking up from my coma, I spent almost two years in Kindred Rehabilitation Hospital in Concord, Massachusetts. After I was discharged, I got my own apartment in Cambridge and lived there for three years. As I was moving into my next apartment, the building I was transitioning into abruptly closed down. Just like that I was facing homelessness.

"The pain, the guilt, and the conflict of leaving one life behind to try to pick up the pieces of another would follow me for years to come."

Thankfully, I gained the wisdom to seek out the VA for help and they steered me toward the Volunteers of America, Massachusetts. My social worker called the program director of the Massachusetts Bay Veteran Center and explained that I needed a place to live.

It is so easy for society not to give a damn about me because I'm black, and I'm a disabled veteran. I use a wheelchair. I don't speak normally due to brain damage that occurred during my stroke. But I feel so very blessed.

It's very easy for people to take advantage of me due to my condition, but Massachusetts Bay Veteran Center did no such thing. The place has truly been a godsend and has far exceeded similar transitional housing and shelters I've stayed at in the past. The center's excellence is a direct reflection of the people in charge. They're not veterans but they want to take care of veterans in need. In a way, they share the same values that informed my service.

With the help of the services provided by Volunteers of America Massachusetts, I'm currently preparing to move into another apartment and am seeking new employment opportunities. I remain connected to my family and my son, who I have been given a second chance with.

Most importantly, I haven't tried to take my own life since God woke me up. This is because I know he has more for me to do. I have no idea what his plan is, but I figure if He had me stay here there's got to be a reason.

I have God, I have my family, I have my son, and I have a future. I am a man renewed. ★

STUART FRANKLIN *is an Army veteran who has proudly served and embraced the veteran community. His story was told to Isaac Oden of Volunteers of America Massachusetts.*

> "God didn't have to let me stay here. But He had other plans."

WHERE IS GOD?

TRACI BLACKMON

It's been more than three years since the killing of Michael Brown Jr. in Ferguson, Missouri. The cameras left long ago and, along with the cameras, many people who diligently followed the story. But the trauma remains, and there has been neither justice nor any effort to acknowledge that wrong was done.

I am a pastor now, but I am also a registered nurse. I know that it takes approximately 66 days to form a habit and slightly longer for behaviors to permanently take hold. It's been more than 660 days since Ferguson, and it's been nearly 600 years since black and brown people have been living under assault in the Americas. That is a long period of enduring hate.

Media bombardment means we who struggle for justice and liberation cannot escape racism, even inside our own homes. Twitter, Facebook, CNN—we are constantly being inundated with stories and news of assaults on somebody, somewhere. So my question is this: What must we do when harm is constant and hate is habitual?

In the context of media bombardment, we've all been called to a difficult task. We are called to see and speak about life in the midst of death, called to seek light in the darkness that surrounds us. Unlike military wars, racism and poverty have not been declared enemies of our collective life, so we are called to fight an undeclared war on the lives of those we love.

We are not qualified for this work because of our supreme righteousness, but because we are intimately familiar with the frailty and flaws of humankind. That frailty is captured in the term moral injury.

What is moral injury? For me, it has two meanings.

I experienced the first meaning after the killing of Michael Brown. I suddenly noticed that generations of young people were missing from the church, young people who were leading the struggle to stop such killings. Worse than their absence was the pain and regret I faced when I acknowledged I hadn't even noticed they were gone. I felt such sorrow. I engaged in lamentation and prayer. Then I took to public repentance for that failure.

That repentance required me to face, and speak openly about, the truth that the death of Michael Brown and others rests on all of our shoulders. If we are to be in solidarity with the struggle, we must face and address the ways in which such violence continues. To become part of the solution, we have to acknowledge that we've been part of the problem too. It doesn't feel good, but it is the truth.

> "We cannot retreat into our sorrow or shame."

I began there, with my awareness of my moral injury and my subsequent repentance. Without that repentance, I do not believe I would have been able to have the relationships that sustain me now. We cannot retreat into our sorrow or shame. We need each other to resist the daily assault on our being—the repetitive wounding of the soul carried in the bodies of those who resist injustice and oppression and who feel the weight of that harm.

Within that struggle is the second meaning of moral injury for me: when authorities betray what is right, when those who are supposed to defend and protect citizens, kill our children instead. When those who are responsible for the common welfare work to reassert white supremacy, they betray us. Such betrayal is acute when we are betrayed by those who claim to care—people who benefit from oppression and do nothing to stop it.

When I used to speak about the cost of inaction, or complicity in oppression, I would say our humanity was at risk. But as I have traveled this path of struggle with so many of its young leaders, I have become increasingly aware that it is not our humanity at risk, it is our divinity—the recognition of the Imago Dei in each of us. Moral injury is damage to our very souls, and the image of God dwells in each of our souls and binds us together.

I learned to think about "God with us" in seminary. But God is not just with us, He is within us. Thinking about how we struggle together in the spirit of truth and of love, I don't have solutions for our moral injuries, but I think we can learn to embrace them. We can take comfort in each other as God with us and be unresolved, be angry, and be hope. Which means, we can be grounded in the Psalm 23 passage that reads, "Yea, though I walk through the valley of the shadow of death, I will fear no evil for thou art with me."

If together we learn to lean into the discomforts of moral injury, to lean into the gaping hole made wide by poverty and racism in this country, we can recognize that God is not present outside of our trauma, but in the midst of it.

It's common for we church folk to think of ourselves as bringing people to God, and of ministers as representing God. But most of the time we're encountering God as He is working elsewhere, so I've been intentional about looking for Him wherever I go, and I found God in Ferguson.

I'm always amused when people ask me, "Where is the church? Why isn't the church here?" I believe that the church emerges rather than being transported to places where it's needed. One of the most healing illustrations of that presence of God comes from a woman called Momma Cat. I share her story with her permission. Momma Cat served in the armed forces, and she and her husband have been a constant presence in Ferguson since the day Michael Brown was killed. One day, in the height of the confrontations between protestors and law enforcement, Momma Cat and her husband showed up at the police station with their truck loaded with long, church-like tables. They took the tables out in the parking lot across from the station, set them with a banquet of food Momma Cat had prepared and served anyone who wanted to eat. The protestors ate; the policemen did not, but they could have. I witnessed healing in that moment because the humanity and divinity of those who had been marginalized was being recognized. It was a way of saying: "You matter."

I don't think anything helps people heal more than knowing they are being seen and heard. It's just that basic. I learned about this from the people in Ferguson. It's experiential learning, and it's proved invaluable to me. It affirmed what I learned in seminary and continue to learn today.

Let us keep looking for God in others. Let us take to the streets where the young people who have left our churches are. We must not become those who we may one day detest because we took comfort in safety and ignorance, and failed to understand that we all live in the valley of the shadow of death. The only way to walk through the valley is to look for God while we are there.

Let us invoke an intentional counter-narrative. Let us seek out people who offer a contradiction to the traumatizing images that are so easy to consume on the news and social media. Let us remain open to encountering God everywhere we go so we no longer fear evil. ★

This essay was adapted from a presentation delivered at The Summit in June 2015. Published with permission from Sojourners.

REV. TRACI BLACKMON *is the Executive Minister of Justice & Local Church Ministries for The United Church of Christ and Senior Pastor of Christ The King United Church of Christ in Florissant, Missouri.*

"I don't have solutions for our moral injuries, but I think we can learn to embrace them."

VERY PRESENT DRAGONS

WAYNE EARL

We connected over our mutual love of journaling. She had a great laugh. I can't pretend to have known her well, but we talked several times over several months. I remember telling her about another young woman her age with whom I once worked but who died recently from a heroin overdose. I remember she listened intently to that story and that it had impact.

But on a cold day in January, after just three months into the residential treatment program where I served as chaplain, she said she wasn't ready to stop using. She abruptly left to spend the weekend with a "38-year-old guy who owned his own business and had his own place."

When someone in the grip of addiction says they aren't ready, I have learned to believe them. The 38-year-old survived. She did not. She was a single mom, an only child, and a beautiful young woman. She was 23 years old.

A few days later another young person in one of our programs—a boy, age 16—told me he desperately wanted to live. He said he wanted to stop the drugs and go to college. He said he was done wasting his time. I believed him.

I left my chaplain job with these stories in my head and threw my hands up in the parking lot, praying out loud. I wondered whether there was anything I could offer people like this, possessed as they were with powers I couldn't pretend to understand.

I sit with them and they look to me for release, asking urgent, simple questions, such as: "Can God help me overcome this/be delivered from this/ be made well/ stop using?" My weak attempt at an answer, if I even have one, is a Jesus-related question: "Do you want to be made whole?"

Psychologists talk about a "locus of control"—a center from which we all make our choices. We either choose from an internal posture or allow some external source to choose for us. We are told that those who have a locus of control that is internally derived tend to be the healthier in our programs, their chances of getting better vastly improved.

As any addict knows, addiction eventually takes any semblance of autonomy, power, and control away. Their helplessness may have sprung from a once-upon-a-time choice not to resist, but that becomes irrelevant once the trap has been set. They now perpetuate a vicious cycle of irresponsible un-choosing. The addict has lost her right to choose. She doesn't need condemnation but rather allies and grace-soaked companions who are resolved to love and linger until the intensity of the spell is loosened, and—better yet—beyond. There is no timetable for this gritty soul work.

> "When someone in the grip of addiction says they aren't ready, I have learned to believe them."

What hope can I offer as a minister to those who feel damned? Sometimes I look into the eyes of these people, and I see death looming and lurking, like a patient, civil, even comfortable, gentleman visitor. It's almost as if he's stopping by for a chat over afternoon tea. But this innocence is a fiction; this is death as non-menace. Once our visitor finds a home, it is simply a matter of time until the invasion is complete. I cannot heal these people. Their deliverance must finally come from within. My job, I think, is in the coaxing. My sword is drawn against dragons that are more real than windmills. I speak truth and life but the healing is not mine. My work is to seduce the Seducer without being seduced.

A few days after my journal-writer friend died, I gathered with the survivors (her friends, mostly young women) to remember her. I told them it was okay to be angry. I told them that no one should die with a needle in their arm, that their friend left a lot undone, and that much good had been lost to the world with her early death. One young lady responded tearfully that she didn't want to dishonor the memory of her friend by turning back to a life of using. She said she would use this tragedy to help in her personal struggle to overcome, one day at a time.

"That's right!" I said.

That's right. This young woman was choosing hope, choosing to live a life before death.

Sometimes as a chaplain I get to share a small part of the joy these amazing people experience when they make a choice to stand and fight, pleading with the universe for just one more good day. And sometimes the beauty slips away too young, too fast. ★

WAYNE EARL, *a Volunteers of America minister, works as a hospital chaplain in Boston, Massachusetts.*

"As any addict knows, addiction eventually takes any semblance of autonomy, power, and control away."

HELPING MYSELF HEAL

WILLIE WEAVER-BEY

My life is a story of ups and downs. I can't remember my mother telling me she loved me when I was a child. But later in life, after I had gone to prison and up until her death, she told me she loved me often. We became very close.

I joined the Army with the hopes of making a career of it, but things didn't turn out as I hoped. When I spurned what I believed to be the sexual advances by a military doctor, I was court martialed and discharged from the Army. It took a lot of therapy for me to open up and talk about this mental sexual trauma, but I find my story helps others heal.

I ended up in prison shortly after my discharge from the Army because my cousin slapped my mother and I shot him. I didn't realize I was suffering from post-traumatic stress disorder at the time.

I felt like I was meant to fail, but God had other plans. The drama of the Army and my prison time left me severely scarred. For years I struggled with an inability to finish anything. I knew I had to find a way to heal. I taught myself to paint in prison and knew it was the only tool I had that might help me.

I was released from prison with $100 and a bus ticket to a city where I didn't know anyone. I didn't know my way around, so I learned the city by riding the bus and walking. During the city bus strike, I sometimes had to walk more than 100 blocks to look for work, then walk the same distance back in time for the halfway house curfew.

Going back to prison was not an option. I slept in a van and took showers at a veterans' help center. Other than the few people who saw me come and go for my daily shower, not many people knew I was homeless. I had a supervisor who used to make fun of my beat-up van; he didn't know the van was my home. I was thankful every day for that van. Despite my inner turmoil, I found a way to stay clean, paint in the back of that cold van and struggle to stay sane.

One of my pieces, "A Veteran, Not Homeless," earned first place at the 2016 National Veterans Creative Arts Festival. Winning the art contest was a positive turning point in my life. I began to heal. More importantly, my story started helping others heal. I am thankful to the VA hospital, Volunteers of America, and all of those who have touched my life and allowed me to share my story. And I am grateful to God for allowing me to be a vessel for him to reach out to others and help them heal physically, emotionally, and spiritually. After forty years of pain and struggle, my gift is that I might inspire one person to have faith and believe they can do what I did and make it in spite of the odds.

Through painting I finally learned how to finish things again. I still cry out of the blue at times, thinking about how good God has been to me and how I am still healing. The odds were against me, but art saved my life. ★

WILLIE WEAVER-BEY *is a custodian for the Clement J. Zablocki VA Medical Center in Milwaukee, and is active in Fresh Perspective, a collective of black male artists in the Milwaukee area.*

> "I had a supervisor who used to make fun of my beat-up van; he didn't know the van was my home."

DISCOVERING MY LIFE'S CALLING

ZELLA RICHARDS

To hear Zella Richard's upbeat voice on the phone, you would have no idea about the rocky road she traveled to get where she is today.

She has been a recovering addict since 1995 and a licensed chemical dependency counselor since 2000. She currently works as a social service coordinator for Volunteers of America Texas, where she helps federal offenders reduce recidivism as they live productively outside of prison. She also eases their fears and helps connect them to the community services they need. When she thinks it will help, she shares her story.

In 1994, Zella went to jail. She weighed just 98 pounds and smoked crack cocaine. She began using drugs and alcohol when she was 15 years old and continued for 17 years. When she was sent to prison, Zella had two children, ages seven and 11. She knew without help for her addiction she would lose her children, and possibly her life.

Her children's father had recently quit using drugs, and he told Zella she should stop too. But his sudden conversion and recommendation that she stop as well seemed sanctimonious to her; it also made her angry because he was the one who introduced her to drugs in the first place. When she looks back on that moment now, however, she knows that his suggestion helped put her on a path to get clean. He passed away of a heart attack the same year she went to prison, and his death devastated her. She found the comfort for her grief and the strength to maintain her sobriety through her faith, the people at the Salvation Army First Choice program, and by attending meetings at Narcotics and Alcoholics Anonymous.

After she was released from prison, Zella sought help from churches. A pastor helped her get admitted into a hospital mental health program where she was diagnosed with depression. Once she was discharged from the hospital, Zella attempted to buy drugs. But she confessed her intentions to her case manager who promptly led Zella to Volunteers of America Texas, to address her addiction. At Volunteers of America, Zella met wonderful people who would become role models for her. Upon successful completion of the Volunteers of America program, Zella was transferred to the Salvation Army First Choice program, which was designed to treat mothers who are addicts and their children.

Zella graduated from the First Choice program but relapsed within 30 days. She attended AA and NA meetings but lied about her sobriety. She wanted to be clean and sober but found her addiction too cunning and powerful. She continued to pray and read the Bible and self-help books, but she also continued to get high.

Finally, almost two years after her prison sentence, Zella turned a corner. She started being honest with herself, her program, and with Jesus, and she started processing and relinquishing her pride, guilt, and shame. She became accountable to her sponsor, who helped her work the 12 steps, and developed a non-using social support system. She also regularly attended AA and NA meetings to acquire effective coping skills to maintain her sobriety. Her motto remains today: "To your own self be true."

Years later, Zella was confronted with another tough situation when her mother had a series of health issues, including stage four lung cancer. As the youngest child, Zella shouldered much of the responsibility in caring for her mother, and she found it an important life-teaching moment. Zella had to teach her mother that it was okay to lean on someone for help, and Zella had to learn to respect her mother's desire to maintain some control in her life.

Zella's recovery from her addiction, and the help she received from Volunteers of America, taught her that having a support system in place is critical. While caring for her mother, Zella relied heavily on her pastor, her church family, and her mentors— all became pillars of strength for her. She learned that you can recover from addictions, but there are life situations that no one can prepare you for, and sometimes the support and skill set you have is not enough.

"She knew without help for her addiction she would lose her children, and possibly her life."

Several months following her cancer diagnosis, Zella's mother passed away. Though devastated, Zella was grateful that her mother had witnessed her daughter's transformation from addiction to recovery. The 12 steps enabled Zella to make amends with her mother and create precious memories without the constraints of unfinished business. Today, Zella holds onto the beautiful memories she shared with her mother throughout her recovery from addiction. "More importantly," she says, "I hold onto the laughter we shared, the lessons I learned, and the wisdom I gained from mom."

Looking back on her life, Zella attributes her strengths and her successes to her faith. She believes that painful events were used to build her character and that Jesus helped her do what she could not do for herself.

Today, Zella has a job with Volunteers of America where she's making a significant difference in the lives of others. "I have a new life," she says. "I want to give back what was freely given to me and to be an example to others who are hurting." ★

ZELLA RICHARDS *is a social service coordinator with Volunteers of America Texas.*

"She wanted to be clean and sober but found her addiction too cunning and powerful."

THE MOMENTUM OF HOPE
A Discussion Guide

In "Continuing the Good Fight," Mike King, president and CEO of Volunteers of America, states, ". . . I never wake up in the morning feeling as if I did everything I could for my mother. Not ever. I never wake up thinking I was a good son." King articulates one of the core issues of moral injury: our judgment that we are not good enough, no matter what we do. When we carry such feelings around with us—guilt, anger, shame, despair—they can take over and isolate us from ourselves, from our loved ones, from our communities, and from our higher power.

Conversely, being able to identify and process inner feelings can help relieve some of our suffering. The essays in this book show how suffering can lead to self-destructive behaviors, loss of faith, and even suicidality. Yet they also show us how—with insight, support, and a rekindling of belief in ourselves and our meaning systems—we can recover from moral injury and help others recover.

Through the questions in this discussion guide, we invite you to examine your understanding and experience of moral injury. As King says, "Let's tackle this. Let's go

deep into this … let's seek out the answers together … Let's ask God to help us …
Let's become the very best … at dealing with moral injury and repairing the deep
damage it does to the soul."

1   **ONE OF THE HALLMARKS OF MORAL INJURY IS DESPAIR AND AN ABSENCE
OF HOPE.** In "A Sense of Place," Harry Quiett says that moral injury is "what
remains when hope has fled and taken with it our sense of self and place—the
things that make us feel worthy of inclusion in the human family and our own
community." In "Healing from Moral Injury," Jon Sherin states that moral injury can
be "crippling and help render the human experience intolerable." Michael Desmond
suggests in "Carrying Our Brothers to Safety" that moral injury is not just about life
or death but also happens when we are forced into combat—or other situations—
where we form deep, necessary bonds and then, when we must leave those bonds,
we receive no understanding or help to process the aftermath. In the resource
section, we also offer clinical definitions of the term. Given all these descriptions,
how would you define moral injury for yourself or to someone else?

2   **ANY PERSON CAN EXPERIENCE MORAL INJURY.** In "Sharing Truth and Healing
Wounds," Angela Arcos describes experiencing domestic violence; Bill Keegan
speaks of moral injury as a first responder during 9/11 in "Hope, Rediscovered."
Veterans, such as Carlos Rodriguez, Jr., Hank Ward, Jim Zenner, Shela Webb, and
Noreen Starr, tell of how serving their country gave rise to morally injurious events.
When you consider their experiences and those you have had or witnessed in your
own life, what types of situations do you believe may give rise to moral injury? Are
there groups of people who may be more likely to experience moral injury?

3   **FAITH AND RELIGION MAY PLAY A SIGNIFICANT ROLE IN MORAL INJURY.**
In "Rediscovering My Soul," Pastor Al Peratt, Sr., talks about making a
commitment to God while in prison to help him find his moral compass again.
In "The Disappearance of My World as I Knew It," retired Volunteers of America
minister Jan Bynum credits her faith—even when she would get angry with
God—with helping her survive the loss of her daughter. Then again, Jim Wallis,
in "All the Children of the World," recounts the ingrained racism he encountered
in 1960s Detroit and a pastor who told him, "Christianity has nothing to do with

racism. Racism is political; our faith is personal." If you are a religious or spiritual person, how have your beliefs either helped sustain you through potentially morally injurious situations or failed you? Has your personal moral code ever conflicted with what you had been taught or with institutional or professional rules? If so, how did you deal with that conflict?

4 **MORAL INJURY HAS BEEN DESCRIBED AS AN IDENTITY CRISIS.** In "Relearning to Live," Hank Ward states that during his tour in Iraq, "We saw things no one should ever see," which may have led to him feeling he had become ". . .someone I still don't recognize." In "Mission: Possible," Orlando Ward talks about losing his identity after a career-ending injury took away the sport that previously defined his life. Many other authors also talk about a sense of losing their identity after a morally injurious event or series of events. Have you ever felt as if you have lost your identity? Having read these accounts, how do you feel moral injury relates to your experiences or to those of people you know?

5 **CAREGIVERS ARE AMONG THE PEOPLE THAT MORAL INJURY SEEMS TO AFFECT DEEPLY BECAUSE CAREGIVING CHALLENGES OUR CAPACITIES FOR LOVE.** In "Are Caregivers Victims of Moral Injury?" Meryl Comer recounts her discomfort with being a "victim" of moral injury as part of caring for her husband with Alzheimer's disease, yet recognizes how caregivers are "invisible to the medical and faith-based communities, even though our own health is being compromised in our service to others." In "Finding a Way Forward," Robert Hopper states, ". . .sometimes I feel like I failed to be the son and caregiver my mother needed and deserved." In "Discovering my Life's Calling," Zella Richards talks about being grateful that her mother lived long enough for Richards to make amends as she provided care to her mother. Have you been a caregiver to a loved one or friend? Is being a caregiver part of your profession? How do you feel moral injury relates to your experiences as a caregiver?

6 **VULNERABLE COMMUNITIES ARE ALSO AT RISK FOR MORAL INJURY.**
Jenni Frumer, in "Moral Injury: A Brief Perspective about the Holocaust," explores its effects on Jewish communities during and after the Holocaust and the secondary trauma experienced by subsequent generations. In "Cheyenne Woman Warrior,"

Noreen Starr considers her personal experiences and the genocide committed against Native Americans in the United States. In "Ferguson and the Spirit of St. Louis: Soul Trauma and Civil Imagination," Rev. Starsky D. Wilson juxtaposes the 250th anniversary celebration of the city while in Ferguson, a young black man bled to death in the street. Rev. Traci Blackmon, in "Where Is God?" urges us all to recognize that to become part of the solution, we must each consider how we are part of the problem. Do you identify as a member of a community that you believe experiences moral injury? Have you experienced moral injury based on your relationship to that community? If so, how do you believe that experience affects your relationship with people both inside and outside that community? Have the ways a community handles moral injury fostered resilience in counteracting its effects?

7 **FOR THOSE STRUGGLING TO RECOVER FROM MORAL INJURY, CONNECTING TO OTHERS AND DEVELOPING A PASSION OR PURPOSE FOR LIVING ARE CRUCIAL.** In "Helping Myself Heal," Willie Weaver-Bey says that "Through painting, I learned to finish things again." In "Guided Forward," Orson Buckmire finds purpose in helping other veterans, while in "Limits and Lifelines," caregiver Mona Hanford speaks of the wonderful advice she received from her priest about putting "lifelines in place" for herself. In "Moral Injury and Marriage," Bobbi L'Huillier describes how the moral injuries experienced separately by a husband and wife can affect the communications and dynamics in their relationship. Shame can keep people from finding connections, but as Rev. Dr. Donald Webb indicates in "Memories of a Minesweeper," it's possible to find a way past shame by helping others. When you consider your connections, who in your life would you talk with about moral injury? How would you approach the subject? How do your connections provide you with resilience for counteracting moral injury's effects?

8 **MANY PEOPLE FEAR BEING RE-TRAUMATIZED OR NOT BEING BELIEVED WHEN THEY TRY TO TALK ABOUT A MORALLY INJURIOUS EVENT.** In "Self-Inflicted Moral Injury," Edward Grinnen recounts his experience as a young man when he committed a violation against his personal moral code that haunted him for many years, yet when he tried to tell his sponsor about it, the sponsor failed to hear him and downplayed the incident as unimportant. In "I Survived," Sharmin Prince states that she never told anyone what had happened to her as a small child until she was

25 years old. Have you ever had an experience you had trouble talking about with anyone? What made it so hard for you?

9 **AN INCREASED RISK FOR COMMITTING SUICIDE IS AMONG MORAL INJURY'S MOST DEVASTATING EFFECTS.** In "A Life with Purpose," the author describes holding a pistol to his head, with only the thought of his son preventing him from pulling the trigger. Carlos Rodriguez, Jr., talks about feeling suicidal after becoming homeless in "On My Way;" in "Pulling the Curtain," Stuart Franklin indicates he attempted suicide on three separate occasions. In "Surviving War and Wondering What If?" Jim Zenner wonders if understanding moral injury better might help prevent suicide in soldiers and veterans. What are the connections that you see between moral injury and suicidality? Do you believe better support for processing moral injury might help prevent some suicides?

10 **MANY APPROACHES AND STRATEGIES HELP RECOVERY FROM MORAL INJURY.** In "Returning to Life," Dr. Rita Brock explores moral injury from a spiritual perspective, recognizing that "our humanity can be exhumed from beneath the outrage, distrust, shame, remorse, guilt, and despair that accompany our moral failures." From a psychologist's perspective in "Stories of Suffering: A Therapist's Approach to Moral Injury," Dr. Bill Gibson describes how he explores moral injury with the veterans with whom he works daily. From his perspective as a psychiatrist, Dr. Jon Sherin suggests a combination of leveraging pharmacology that promotes neural flexibility and therapeutic approaches that can bring about healing. From his place on the front lines with addicted youth, Wayne Earl believes that he cannot condemn those who feel damned, "My work is to seduce the Seducer without being seduced." As you consider the various ways recovery from moral injury can happen, which of these approaches resonates for you? What other approaches might you recommend? How do you think talking to a therapist, religious leader, or peer who has recovered could help you or someone you know begin to address moral injury? How might talking to a trusted friend or family member help? ★

MORAL INJURY RESOURCES

The resources provided here are not exhaustive but do provide unique perspectives on various aspects of moral injury.

CLINICAL DEFINITIONS

1   Shay, Jonathan (2014). Moral Injury. *Psychoanalytic Psychology*. American Psychological Association Vol. 31, No. 2, 182–191.
    "Moral injury is present when there has been (a) a betrayal of 'what's right'; (b) either by a person in legitimate authority (my definition), or by one's self—'I did it' (Litz, Maguen, Nash, et al.); (c) in a high stakes situation."

2   Litz, Brett T.; Stein Nathan; Delaney, Eileen; Lebowitz, Leslie; Nash, William P.; Silva, Caroline; and Maguen, Shira (2009). Moral Injury and Moral Repair in War Veterans: A Preliminary Model and Intervention Strategy. *Clinical Psychology Review, 29, 695–706.*
    "Perpetrating, failing to prevent, bearing witness to, or learning about acts that transgress deeply held moral beliefs and expectations."

3   Drescher, K.D., Foy, D. W., Kelly, C., Leshner, A., Schutz, K. (2011). An Exploration of the Viability and Usefulness of the Construct of Moral Injury in War Veterans. *Traumatology.* 17, 1, 8–13.
    Drescher, Kent D. and Foy, David W. (2008). When They Come Home: Post-Traumatic Stress, Moral Injury, and Spiritual Consequences for Veterans. *Reflective Practice: Formation and Supervision in Ministry, 28,* 85–102.
    "Disruption in an individual's confidence and expectations about one's own or others' motivation or capacity to behave in a just and ethical manner."

4   Knowles, C. (2013). Notes toward a Neuropsychology of Moral Injury. *Reflective Practice: Formation and Supervision in Ministry.* vol. 33. Available at: http://journals.sfu.ca/rpfs/index.php/rpfs/article/view/265/264. Accessed January 25, 2017.

5   Tangley, J. P., Stuewig, J., Mashek, D. J. Moral Emotions and Moral Behavior. *Annual Rev. Psychol.* 2007; 58: 345–372.

RESOURCES

WEBSITES

The Moral Injury Project. moralinjuryproject.syr.edu.

Soul Repair Center. brite.edu/academics/programs/soul-repair

Veterans Affairs PTSD website article on moral injury. www.ptsd. va.gov/professional/newsletters/research-quarterly/v23n1.pdf.

Volunteers of America. www.voa.org/moral-injury

BOOKS

Nonfiction

Bica, C. M. (2016). *The moral casualties of war.* Gnosis Press.

Brock, R. N. and Lettini, G. (2012). *Soul repair: Recovering from moral injury after war.* Beacon Press. Study guide for book groups: https://www.brite.edu/wp-content/uploads/2013/07/Soul-Repair-Book-Study-Guide-March-20141.pdf.

Busch, B. (2012). *Dust to dust: A memoir.* Ecco Press.

Casteel, J. (2008). *Letters from Abu Ghraib.* Essay Press.

Decety, J. and Ickes, W. eds. (2011). *The social neuroscience of empathy.* MIT Press.

Frankl, V. (1946) *Man's Search for Meaning.* Beacon Press.

Goodell J. and Hearn, J. E. (2011). *Shade it black: Death and after in Iraq.* Casemate Pub.

Grossman, D. (1996). *On killing: The psychological cost of learning to kill in war and society.* Back Bay Books.

Graham, L. (2017). *Moral injury: Restoring wounded souls.* Abingdon.

Harris, T.W. (2015) *The sisters are alright: Changing the broken narrative of black women in America.* Berrett-Koehler Publishers.

Litz, B. T.; Lebowitz, L.; Gray, M. J.; and Nash, W. P. (2015). *Adaptive disclosure: A new treatment for military trauma, loss, and moral injury.* Guilford.

Marlantes, K. (2011). *What it is like to go to war.* Atlantic Monthly Press.

McDonald, J. (2017). Ed. *Exploring moral injury in sacred texts.* Philadelphia, PA: Jessica Kingsley Publishers.

Meagher, R. E. (2015). Killing from the inside out: Moral injury and just war. Cascade Books.

Meagher, R. E. and Pryer, D. A., eds. (2018). *War and Moral Injury: A Reader.* Eugene, OR: Cascade Books.

Miller, Ronald B. (2004). *Facing human suffering: Psychology and psychotherapy as moral engagement.* Washington, DC: American Psychological Association.

Moon, Z. (2015). *Coming home: Ministry that matters with veterans and military families.* Chalice Press.

Peters, D. (2016) *Post-traumatic god: How the church cares for people who have been to hell and back.* Morehouse Publ.

Santiago, E. (1933) *When I was Puerto Rican.* Vintage Books.

Shay, Jonathan (1995). *Achilles in Vietnam: Combat trauma and the undoing of character.* Simon and Schuster.

Shay, Jonathan (2002). *Odysseus in America: Combat trauma and the trials of homecoming.* Scribner.

Sherman, Nancy (2015). *Afterwar: Healing the moral wounds of our soldiers.* Oxford University Press.

Sites, Kevin (2013). *The things they cannot say: Stories soldiers won't tell you about what they've seen, done, or failed to do in war.* Harper Perennial.

Tick, Edward (2014). *Warrior's return: Restoring the soul after war.* Sounds True.

Van Der Kolk, B. (2014) *The body keeps the score: Brain, mind, and body in the healing of trauma.* Penguin.

Verkamp, B. (2005). *Moral treatment of returning warriors in early medieval and modern times.* Univ. of Scranton.

Wood, David (2016). *What have we done? The moral injury of our longest wars.* Little, Brown, & Co.

Fiction

Alvarez, J. (1991) *How the Garcia girls lost their accents*. Workman Publishing Company.

Gay, R. (2017) *Difficult women*. Grove Press.

Klay, P. (2014). *Redeployment*. Penguin Books.

Marlantes, K. (2010). *Matterhorn: A novel of the Vietnam War*. Atlantic Monthly Press.

O'Brien, T. (1990). *The things they carried*. Houghton-Mifflin.

Powers, K. (2012). *The yellow birds*. Little, Brown, & Co.

Whitehead, C. (2016) *The underground railroad*. Doubleday

Journal Articles & Book Chapters

Boudreau, T. (2011). The morally injured. *Massachusetts Review*. 52, 3/4, 746–54.

Brock, R. N. (2015). Post-traumatic stress, moral injury, and soul repair: The implications of Western Christian theology. *Issues in Science and Theology: Do Emotions Shape the World?* Evers, D., Fuller, M., Runehov, A., and Sæther, K., eds. Edinburgh, Scotland. Springer Press, vol. 3: 27–40.

Carten, A. (July 27, 2015) How slavery's legacy affects the mental health of black Americans. *The New Republic*.

Gibbons-Neff, Thomas (March 6, 2015). "Haunted by their decisions in war." *Washington Post*.

Kirkpatrick, Jesse (January 26, 2016). "Military drone operators risk a serious injury." *Slate*.

Mejia, C. E. (2011). Healing moral injury: A lifelong journey: But what does that mean? *Fellowship*. Vol. 76, Iss. 10–12: 25–27.

Puniewska, Maggie (July 3, 2015). "Healing a wounded sense of morality." *The Atlantic*.

Ramchand, R. (2011). The war within: Preventing suicide within the military. Washington D.C. Rand Corporation.

Shepard, Aaron Pratt (December 9, 2017) "For veterans, a path to healing 'moral injury'." *New York Times*.

Sonya B.; Wilkins, Kendall C.; Meyers, Ursula S.; and Allard, Carolyn B. (2014). Trauma informed guilt reduction therapy with combat veterans. *Cognitive Behavioral Practice*, 21(1), 76–88.

Powers, B. (2017). Moral injury and original sin: The applicability of Augustinian moral psychology in light of combat trauma. *Theology Today*. 73(4). 325–337.

Price, June T.; Steuwig, Jeff; and Mashek, Debra (2007). *Moral emotions and moral behavior*. Annual Review of Psychology, *58*, 345–272.

DOCUMENTARIES

Ground truth. Directed by Patricia Foulkrod. United States: Focus Features, 2006.

The invisible war. Directed by Kerby Dick. Cinedigm Docurama Films, 2012. DVD.

Lioness. Directed by Meg McLagan and Daria Sommers. Room 11 Productions, 2008.

Restrepo. Directed by Tim Hetherington and Sebastian Junger. National Geographic Entertainment, 2010. DVD.

Soldiers of conscience. Directed by Catherine Ryan and Gary Weimberg. Luna Productions, 2007.

Taxi to the dark side. Directed by Alex Gibney. Think Film, 2007.

Korengal. Directed by Sebastian Junger. Outpost Films, 2014. DVD.

After fire. Directed by Brittany Huckabee, Odyssey Productions, 2016.

Almost sunrise. Directed by Michael Collins. Veterans Trek Productions LLC., 2017.

The PBS Ken Burns/Lynn Novick Series, "The Vietnam War". See https://www.voa.org/a-guide-to-hosting-compassionate-conversations-about-moral-injury-and-the-documentary-the-vietnam-war for a guide to compassionate conversations about the war.

FILMS

The best years of our lives (1946) — Combat trauma and moral injury in WW II veterans

Coming home (1978) — Combat trauma and moral injury in Vietnam veterans

The deerhunter (1978) — Combat trauma and moral injury in Vietnam veterans

The accused (1988) — Noncombat PTSD and moral injury from sexual assault

Born on the Fourth of July (1989) — Combat trauma and moral injury in Vietnam veterans

Jackknife (1989) — Combat trauma and moral injury in Vietnam veterans

The fisher king (1991) — Noncombat PTSD

The prince of tides (1991) — Adult effects of childhood trauma, moral injury (suicidality)

Schindler's list (1993) — Noncombat moral injury

The war at home (1996) — Combat trauma and moral injury in Vietnam veterans

Missing in America (2005) — Combat trauma and moral injury in Vietnam veterans

Gran Torino (2008) — Combat trauma and moral injury in Korean War veterans

In the valley of Elah (2008) — Combat trauma and moral injury in OED/OIF/OND veterans

Stop-loss — Combat trauma and moral injury in OED/OIF/OND troops, 2008.

Brothers (2009) — Combat trauma and moral injury in OED/OIF/OND veterans

Manchester by the sea (2016) — Noncombat moral injury

Get out (2017) — A black man who uncovers a disturbing secret when he meets the family of his white girlfriend

Three billboards outside Ebbing, Missouri (2017) — Noncombat moral injury

AUDIO

Moral injury: The psychological wounds of war. NPR Talk of the Nation. Nov. 21, 2012. https://www.npr.org/2012/11/21/165663154/moral-injury-the-psychological-wounds-of-war.

The moral injury vets bring home: Interview with David Wood. The Brian Lehrer Show. April 2, 2014. https://www.wnyc.org/story/moral-injuries-veterans/.

Conversation with Karl Marlantes: Interview by Steve Kraske, NPR. Nov. 11, 2015. http://kcur.org/post/author-and-former-marine-moral-injury-war#stream/0.

VIDEOS

Truth commission on conscience in war testimonies (2010). Tyler Boudreau. https://www.youtube.com/watch?v=F5uaMwZVhwQ. (10 min)

The war within: A veteran's struggle with moral injury. Michael Yandell. Oct. 14, 2014. https://www.youtube.com/watch?v=Ex_2pS6Ekkk. (20 min)

Torture, trauma, and the moral injuries of war. (2015). Bill Edmonds, Clark University, November 12, 2015. (30 min) https://www.youtube.com/watch?v=qVdcOeWsI0E&feature=youtu.be

Moral injury: The hidden legacy of war. Rita N. Brock. August 2016. https://www.youtube.com/watch?v=y4OoWPGYykc. (75 min)

What is moral injury? William Nash. September 2017. https://www.youtube.com/watch?v=k6JxbtFiYhg. (10 min)

THANK YOU HSBC

VOLUNTEERS OF AMERICA WISHES TO THANK HSBC for its generous support of *The Momentum of Hope* and our efforts to provide veterans with supportive services, housing, employee and vocational training, and healing. For 153 years, HSBC has connected developed countries with developing countries with the goal of helping everyone, everywhere to achieve a dream of prosperity. One way the bank helps people to achieve that prosperity is by investing in leading nonprofit organizations who are focused on employability and financial capabilities, and who empower entrepreneurs and businesses. In the United States, HSBC's commitment to hiring veterans has yielded positive results—more than doubling the number of veteran hires at the company in 2017. HSBC continues this important work with programs such as Veterans on Wall Street (VOWS), and its "Military Path" hiring which earmarks key roles for veteran candidate slates. There is a vital partnership at HSBC between its VALOR Employee Resource Group, and its Recruitment and Learning functions. This enables HSBC to provide an holistic approach to the attraction, hiring , onboarding, and retaining of veterans. Find out more at hsbc.com.

HSBC's generous support has been invaluable in helping Volunteers of America move forward on expanding and enhancing the services we provide to veterans, including our moral injury initiative. With their help, we launched a multi-year initiative to expand wraparound services for veterans, especially vulnerable veterans in targeted high-risk, high-need communities.

On behalf of all the people we serve, thank you.

ABOUT VOLUNTEERS OF AMERICA

VOLUNTEERS OF AMERICA IS A MINISTRY OF SERVICE dedicated to helping those in need rebuild their lives and reach their full potential. Through hundreds of human service programs, including housing and health care, Volunteers of America helps almost 1.3 million people in more than 400 communities across the United States each year. Volunteers of American has launched a new initiative to help provide relief and a means to recovery for those suffering from moral injury. Learn more at voa.org.

PHOTOGRAPHY CREDITS

Page 14: Brandon Thibodeaux / *The New York Times* / Redux; page 46: threerocksimages /
Shutterstock.com; page 49: Glynnis Jones / Shutterstock.com; page 75: deviangel / Shutterstock.com;
page 91, top: Yakovlev Sergey / Shutterstock.com; page 91, bottom: Oliver Foerstner /
Shutterstock.com; page 102: Dan MacMedan; page 161: Wiley Price, *The St. Louis American*;
page 167: Sean Locke Photography / Shutterstock.com; page 173: Gino Santa Maria / Shutterstock.com;
pages 178, 181: Pat A. Robinson, *Milwaukee Journal Sentinel*

Library of Congress Control Number: 2018903930

ISBN-13: 978-0692099810 (Volunteers of America)
ISBN-10: 0692099816

FOR VOLUNTEERS OF AMERICA
Jatrice Martel Gaiter, Co-Editor
Douglas McAllister, Co-Editor

Editing by Terri Sapienza
Design by Sarah Gifford

Volunteers of America
1660 Duke Street
Alexandria, VA 22314
www.voa.org

PRINTED IN THE UNITED STATES

Made in the USA
Lexington, KY
23 April 2018